Freedom and Its Misuses:

Kierkegaard on Anxiety and Dispair

Gregory R. Beabout

MARQUETTE
UNIVERSITY
PRESS

Library of Congress Cataloging-in-Publication Data

Beabout, Gregory R., 1960-
  Freedom and its misuses : Kierkegaard on anxiety and despair /
Gregory R. Beabout.
    p.   cm. — (Marquette studies in philosophy ; #12)
  Includes bibliographical references and index.
  ISBN 0-87462-612-9 (pbk.)
    1. Kierkegaard, Søren, 1813-1855—Contributions in philosophical
concept of self. 2. Self (Philosophy) 3. Free will and
determinism. 4. Liberty. 5. Anxiety. 6. Despair. 7. Kierkegaard,
Søren, 1813-1855. Syldommen til døden. I. Title. II. Series.
  B4378.S4B33   1996
  198'.9—dc20   95.50161

Printed in the United States of America
© 1996 Marquette University Press

MARQUETTE UNIVERSITY PRESS
MILWAUKEE

The Association of Jesuit University Presses

Contents

Acknowledgements

There are many people and institutions that I would like to thank for their influence and help, both direct and indirect, on this book. I have benefited from many fine teachers. While an undergraduate at Loyola University Chicago, my teachers and friends helped me think about the question of freedom and what it means to be a human being. In graduate school, Thomas Anderson introduced me to the serious study of Kierkegaard and helped refine my questions about the meaning of freedom. Howard Kainz encouraged me in the study of Kierkegaard as well. Many people have read drafts of this manuscript in various stages, and I have often borrowed their suggestions. I would like to thank especially Eileen Sweeney, Michael Vater, Walter Stohrer, Daryl Wennemann and Michael Wreen for their comments. Twice I spent time at the Howard and Edna Hong Kierkegaard Library at St. Olaf's in Northfield, Minnesota. These visits were fruitful, both because of the well organized research facilities at the library and the environment that encouraged reflection. In 1988 I received a Smith Fellowship and in 1992 I was awarded a Saint Louis University Faculty Development Grant. I am grateful for this support. At

St. Olaf's, I benefitted from conversations with C. Stephen Evans and the Hongs, as well as from the help of Cynthia Lund and others. I would like to thank my research assistants, John Morris and Nicholas Plants. Andy Tallon has been a great support in many capacities, both in reading and commenting on the text and especially as editor. My greatest debt in this book, at least with regard to a direct influence for my thinking, is to John D. Jones. Always willing to engage me as an individual with questions, this project grew out of our very slow and careful reading of Kierkegaard, much of which occurred in his living room. The central question of the book arose while we were walking and talking together at the park near his house. Through his ability to question, to probe, and to encourage, his positive influence permeates this book far more than might be recognized. In gratitude, this book is dedicated to him. Of course, there is the far different kind of debt I owe to my family—my parents, grandparents, and especially my wife. Not only am I grateful for the endless hours she spent listening to me work out my ideas, patiently listening as I read draft after draft, but for the loving support that comes only in a family.

G.R.B. *St. Louis*
Thanksgiving, 1995

Foreword

This small and solid work is everything one hopes for in a book on Kierkegaard. It treats him as both a great thinker and a corrective to our time and is both scholarly and popular in the best sense of those terms. For Kierkegaard scholars it provides detailed and careful accounts of his key concepts of anxiety and despair, comments on much of the existing secondary literature on these topics, provides many helpful etymological insights and even contains a perceptive and generously noted use of my own *Indices*. It also does nice things like distinguishing between the "lower pseudonymous works," the "upbuilding works," and the "higher pseudonymous works." It shows why Sartre is no match for Kierkegaard, why and how Alasdair MacIntyre has misrepresented him so badly and why finally Freud has nothing to say about human freedom. For the general reader it explains the radical significance of these Kierkegaardian concepts for our understanding of freedom and shows how they might yet serve to salvage a dream gone obviously and terribly wrong. I suspect that an equally careful treatment of the relevant texts would show that Kierkegaard is not an "individualist" but Professor Beabout has done a great deal to clarify and connect anxiety, despair and freedom and those who care about humanity can profit greatly from his labors.

Almost by accident I began reading this work late on Good Friday evening and finished it at noon on Saturday but in retrospect perhaps this was a mistake. Its publication is an occasion for joy and hope and no doubt I should have left the end until Easter morning.

Alastair McKinnon
Søren Kierkegaard Research Centre
McGill University
Easter, 1995

To John D. Jones

With thanks
for encouragement and direction

The age is liberal, broadminded, and philosophical; the sacred claims of personal liberty have everywhere a host of appreciated and applauded spokesmen. Nevertheless, it seems to me that the case is not always apprehended in a sufficiently dialectical manner . . .

Søren Kierkegaard

You were called to be free. But do not let this freedom become an excuse to let your desires control you.

St. Paul

ABBREVIATIONS

The following abbreviations of works by Kierkegaard will
be used.

CA	*The Concept of Anxiety*
CDisc	*Christian Discourses*
CDread	*The Concept of Dread (Lowrie Translation)*
CUP	*Concluding Unscientific Postscript to the Philosophical Fragments*
ED	*Edifying Discourses*
E/O I, II	*Either/Or, volumes I and II*
FT	*Fear and Trembling*
GS	*The Gospel of Suffering*
Pap.	*Søren Kierkegaard's Papier*
PF	*Philosophical Fragments*
PH	*Purity of Heart is to Will One Thing*
PV	*The Point of View for My Work as an Author*
R	*Repetition*
SKJP	*Søren Kierkegaard's Journals and Papers*
SLW	*Stages on Life's Way*
SUD	*The Sickness Unto Death*
TC	*Training in Christianity*

CHAPTER 1
Introduction

Freedom continues to be perhaps the most important concept in modern and post-modern society. It was the central idea in the revolution of 1789, as well as in the revolutions of 1989. In France, the accent in the rallying cry *Liberté! Égalité! Fraternité!* was freedom, freedom, freedom. Two hundred years later, the students in Tiananman Square quoted the enlightenment thinkers on freedom, and held Lady Liberty high in their parade. In the fall of the same year, Germans chanted "freedom, freedom" with each concrete splintering swing that cracked and destroyed the Iron Curtain at the Brandenburg Gate. But freedom was not universally praised in 1989, and especially not in the land of the free. The year 1989 brought social unrest in the United States as protesters marched with Operation Rescue, chaining themselves to abortion clinics to criticize free choice gone astray. Likewise, others protested against lewd art exhibits, voicing "this is not what freedom means." Flag wavers and flag burners debated an issue that is tacitly centered around an apparent inherent paradox in the meaning of freedom: In a free society, should it be legal to burn the symbol of freedom? Hence, 1989 was a year that typified the contemporary age, of social unrest throughout the world, of dissension encouraged by the taste of freedom. But while protesters in China and East Germany shouted for freedom's sweet fragrance, protesters in the United States complained that after 200 years, liberty had gone sour. In the States, freedom, that grand idea, the cornerstone of democracy, had led not to a society where we exalt responsibility, but to the legal burning of flags, to an epidemic of teenage abortions, to the celebration of being able to place a crucifix in a cup of one's own urine.

The understanding of the concept of freedom that has shaped the modern world is one that comes out of the enlightenment. Freedom is understood to mean "being able to do whatever you want." Freedom's scope is wide. As Walker Percy writes, we seek freedom's promise to be "liberated by education from the traditional bonds of religion, by democracy from the strictures of class, by technology from the drudgery of poverty, and by self-knowledge from the tyranny of the unconscious" so that each of us are left to do whatever we want (1983, 17). Freedom's promise, that one will no longer be enslaved to ignorance, social expectations, the church, the state, poverty or even uncontrollable drives, is a Faustian bargain. For freedom promises freedom from enslavement, but in exchange it offers the freedom not to be oneself, and ultimately to become self-enslaved.

Left with freedom's promise and no clear blueprint as to what to do with it, freedom becomes enslavement. The enlightenment promise of the freedom to pursue happiness however one sees fit is transformed from a life of work, family, the marketplace, the political process, cultural activities, sports, the sciences and the arts to a life óf day time game shows and the daily lotto, or to the sophisticated but shallow connoisseurship of aging yuppies, or to late night cynics who stand one step removed from life to laugh at its folly, or to angry and lonely defiance. The walk of life that freedom holds out as a promise is transformed into a gnawing dissatisfaction, one that becomes more tormenting each time it should become less so.

What is needed, at least to begin, is a deeper understanding of the meaning of freedom. The enlightenment concept of freedom, "to be able to do whatever you want," has several shortcomings. These flaws, made evident by the frustrations of the twentieth century, stem principally from the attempt to define freedom without an adequate understanding of the human self.

If the central concept of antiquity was justice, its greatest expression came in Plato's *Republic*. The genius of the *Republic* is that its central question is really three questions. "What is justice?" is answered by asking "what is the just state?" But that question hides the real underlying question: "what is the just soul?" So the overriding issue, the attempt to understand the meaning of justice, is transformed into an attempt to describe the perfect state. Yet when read carefully, when Plato's irony is understood, we realize that the state described is not really an account of the perfect state, for there is no room for Socrates in Plato's republic, since there is no room for a gadfly in the state of philosopher kings. The driving question of the *Republic* is not about the state, but about the soul. The description of the just state is a metaphor for the description of the just soul, as a correct understanding of justice flows not from an abstract consideration of fairness and equality, but from a concrete examination of the human soul.

Likewise, if the central concept of modernity is freedom, an adequate account of freedom should have its roots in an examination of the human self. To understand freedom more fully, we need to see that the question of freedom has moved beyond the socio-political question of being free from capricious governmental leaders, to deeper psychological, metaphysical and religious questions. Further, we need to move beyond the traditional freedom/determinism debate, for that debate only makes sense within an inadequate understanding of the human self. If the self is taken to be a thinking thing standing outside of the physical world, then the self is radically free, but with a freedom that is indifferent to concrete existence. On the other hand, if the self is taken to be simply one more item in the environment, only quantitatively different from other organisms that can be scientifically accounted for, then the environment determines us. Therefore, the debate about freedom implies a debate about metaphysics, a debate about two inadequate views of the self. The one view of the self denies the concrete facticity of every day life, and the other tacitly denies the ability to transcend the environment through language, memory and imagination. Hence, if we are to seek a better understand of freedom, to probe not only its socio-political meaning but also its psychological, ontological and religious significance, we need a better understanding of the self.

Søren Kierkegaard began this task for us. Widely recognized as one of the most influential thinkers of the nineteenth century, as one of the forerunners of the philosophy of existentialism, and as one who shaped neo-orthodox protestant theology, there remain problems in understanding Kierkegaard and his contribution to the meaning of freedom.

Though freedom is perhaps the central concern of Kierkegaard's work, he never wrote a book titled "The Concept of Freedom." He might have had he lived longer. Other books of his focused on conceptual clarification; his dissertation was *The Concept of Irony* and he wrote *The Concept of Anxiety*. But Kierkegaard does not offer us a single book devoted solely to an understanding of freedom. Instead, to understand his philosophy of freedom, first we need to draw out his ideas from his psychological works and lay bare his understanding of the human self, and then we can get a sense of his account of human freedom. That is my task.

1. The Purpose of this Work

My purpose in this book is to shed light on the meaning of human freedom, that is, of entangled freedom, by examining and making clear the relationship between the concepts of anxiety and despair in the writings of Søren Kierkegaard.

Kierkegaard's life, which lasted from 1813-55, was quiet enough. Still, because he so brilliantly described his inner moods and thoughts in his journals, there has been a temptation to interpret Kierkegaard's writing strictly through his life, to reduce his psychological writings to an expression of his own melancholy. I think that this is wrongheaded, even to the point that I would say that Kierkegaard's works on anxiety and despair might be better understood without focusing on his life. Nevertheless, for those interested, an account of Kierkegaard's life can be found in most of the standard introductions to Kierkegaard, and reading his journals is as voyeuristically interesting as reading a lost diary, especially if one suspects that the owner intentionally lost the diary hoping that you would find it and read it.

What we can learn from Kierkegaard about the self and freedom does not depend so much on his melancholy, on his brooding disposition, on his ability to record his experiences of anxiety and despair in his life, as it depends on his ability to show how ordinary enough feelings such as anxiety and despair reveal a deeper account of the human self and of human freedom.

Anxiety and despair, therefore, are central to Kierkegaard's conception of the self and freedom. He discusses them principally in two works, *The Concept of Anxiety*, published in 1844, and *The Sickness Unto Death*, written in 1848 but published in 1849. As we will see, anxiety and despair each has a complex structure and both are closely interrelated to one another. This thematic interconnection between anxiety and despair is doubled and made more difficult by the textual relationship between the two works and the fact that they have different pseudonymous "authors." Further, both these works are very dense and bristle with problems of meaning and interpretation. Therefore, my task will involve a careful articulation of the structure and relation between anxiety and despair through a close textual analysis of *The Concept of Anxiety* and *The Sickness Unto Death*.

It is widely held by translators and commentators that there is a close affinity between *The Concept of Anxiety* and *The Sickness Unto Death*. Among translators for example, Howard Hong writes that *The Concept of Anxiety* and *The Sickness Unto Death* "may be regarded as a two-stage explication. Both are based on the concept of man as a synthesis of the finite and the infinite, the temporal and the eternal" (*SUD*, xi). Reidar Thomte holds the two works belong together inasmuch as both "consider the anthropological aspects of freedom" (*CA*, viii). Lowrie also points out the similitude between the two works.[1]

In the same manner, Kierkegaard commentators have grouped the two works together. Gregor Malantschuk writes "*The Sickness Unto Death* may be looked upon as a continuation of *The Concept of Anxiety*" (1971, 339). Vincent McCarthy agrees, calling the latter a dialectical continuation of the earlier work (1978, 82). Kresten Nordentoft claims that "from a psychological point of view, there are two of Kierkegaard's works which are especially significant, *The Concept of Anxiety* and *The Sickness Unto Death*" (1972, xx). Paul Tillich also groups together the two works. He writes "There are two writings which every theologian must read. Both are comparatively short: The Concept of [Anxiety] and *The Sickness Unto Death*" (1967, 166). Thus the close affinity between the two works is commonly recognized, even though Kierkegaard wrote many books during the years between the publication of these two.

There are other reasons why Kierkegaard's books on anxiety and despair should be considered together. In both, Kierkegaard develops his view of the self. Both works are similar in that in both cases, Kierkegaard nearly signed his name as author of the works, but shortly before publication, he assigned a pseudonym to each. While many of his other works were written with the intention of being pseudonymous, these two are similar in that their pseudonymity was an afterthought. Both seek to clarify concepts essential to Kierkegaard's psychology. Further, both anxiety and despair are affective states or moods that Kierkegaard sees as being based in ontological structures of being human. Even more, he also uses these terms, which normally refer to affects, to refer to the ontological structures in which the affects are based. Finally, there is an important sense in which *The Concept of Anxiety* is incomplete without *The Sickness Unto Death*. In *The Concept of Anxiety*, the term sin is repeatedly employed without ever being clarified. What Kierkegaard means by sin is only made clear with his explanation of the concept of despair in *The Sickness Unto Death*.

In order to understand the self, Kierkegaard examines not human rationality (as had many earlier philosophers) but feelings and moods, freedom and individuality. This approach has been widely influential, especially in our century, the age of anxiety. Martin Heidegger drew heavily upon Kierkegaard's concept of anxiety (1962, 228-235). The themes of anxiety and despair are important in the thought of Sartre, Jaspers and Unamuno. Similarly, the themes of anxiety and despair are important for both Niebuhr and Tillich. Kierkegaard's concept of anxiety influenced the work of psychologist Rollo May. Ernest Becker calls Kierkegaard a "post-Freudian," arguing that though his work was not widely recognized in the 19th century, the psychological insights push beyond Freud (1973). Other writers see Kierkegaard as the first post-modernist, anticipating Derrida.[2] But despite the attention that Kierkegaard's work has received, the relationship between anxiety and despair is still not clearly understood, and neither are the insights about human freedom that this relationship implies.

2. Interpretations of the Relationship

Though there are no major secondary works that focus primarily on the relationship between anxiety and despair in Kierkegaard's thought, there are a number of authors who make mention of the relationship while discussing some other topic. These can be reduced to four basic interpretations.

(1) The most explicitly worked out view on the connection between anxiety and despair is that of Gregor Malantschuk. He sees a connection between the works on anxiety and despair, though he does not correctly formulate the connection.

> The Sickness Unto Death may be looked upon as a continuation of The Concept of Anxiety. Since The Concept of Anxiety begins on the lowest level with the portrayal of the human situation and the resulting forms of the misrelation in the synthesis expressed in anxiety, and since The Sickness Unto Death deals with the higher forms of this misrelation, these two books are best suited to demonstrate the continuous dialectical line which also runs through the other books in Kierkegaard's authorship but come out particularly in these two books with all the clarity and convincing power one could wish (Malantschuk 1971, 339)

Malantschuk views both anxiety and despair as being misrelations in the individual. He sees anxiety as the misrelation at the lower levels of human existence; he claims that when the eternal, and hence the spiritual, in the individual is excluded, the misrelation is anxiety. To support this, he claims that in The Concept of Anxiety, the eternal in man has been bracketed from the discussion. Malantschuk writes "the domain of anxiety lies within the scope of man's mental-physical synthesis" (1971, 339). Hence, his position is that Kierkegaard views anxiety as a misrelation in the self at the mental-physical level. Conversely, with the inclusion of the spiritual element, the misrelation in the individual is despair. "If in *The Concept of Anxiety* Vigilius Haufniensis [the pseudonymous author] had taken into consideration the factor of the eternal in man, he would have come upon the category of despair as well as the category of anxiety" (1971, 340). Malantschuk's view, then, is that anxiety and despair are both misrelations in the self. He takes anxiety to be the misrelation at the mental-physical level before the spiritual element is actualized, and on his view, despair is the misrelation in the self after the spiritual element is actualized.

This interpretation is inadequate for two reasons. First, it makes anxiety out to be a misrelation in the self, whereas for Kierkegaard, anxiety is not itself a misrelation. Second, Malantschuk claims that anxiety occurs only at the mental-physical level and not at the spiritual level. But for Kierkegaard in *The Concept of Anxiety*, anxiety can occur at the spiritual level.[3]

Despite these problems with this interpretation of the relationship between anxiety and despair, several authors follow Malantschuk on the relation between anxiety and despair, or hold some closely related variation. The author of the back cover of the Hong translation of *The Sickness Unto Death* writes:

> In *The Sickness Unto Death*, Kierkegaard moves beyond anxiety on the mental-emotional level to the spiritual level, where—in contact with the eternal—anxiety becomes despair. Both anxiety and despair reflect the misrelation that arises in the self when the elements of the synthesis—he infinite and the finite—do not come into proper relation to each other. Despair is a deeper expression for

anxiety and is a mark of the eternal, which is intended to penetrate temporal existence.

Vincent A. McCarthy explicitly follows Malantschuk on the relation between anxiety and despair, and goes even further; he claims that despair is the "intensified form" of anxiety (1978, 84-85). Robert Perkins seems to maintain the same view when he writes that anxiety is "transmuted into despair" and "anxiety is raised to a new level of intensity in despair" (1969, 30). John Hoberman does not explicitly claim that despair is an intensification of anxiety, but his interpretation of the relationship between the two concepts is similar, since he claims that anxiety is a "psychological (and ultimately, religious) disorientation" (1987, 185). This tends toward the Malantschuk view, that anxiety is a misrelation that intensifies and develops into the sickness of despair.

It is unclear what is meant by claiming that despair is an intensification of anxiety. If we take an intensification to be a change in degree without being a change in kind, then this view is problematic, since this would ultimately disregard the qualitative leap of the individual into sin. In other words, to say that despair is an intensification of anxiety is tantamount to saying that despair is only quantitatively different from anxiety. This interpretation ends up missing Kierkegaard's point about choice and responsibility.[4]

All of these commentators make anxiety out to be a low level of despair. As we will see, this view is understandable, since there is a passage in *The Sickness Unto Death* in which Anti-Climacus loosely equates anxiety and despair (*SUD*, 22). However, I will show that Anti-Climacus is not there using the term "anxiety" in the developed technical sense in which Vigilius Haufniensis uses the term in *The Concept of Anxiety*.[5] In the technical sense developed in *The Concept of Anxiety* anxiety is an ontological structure in which the self is both attracted to and repulsed from the nothingness of future possibilities. Anxiety is not a misrelation in the self.

(2) Another view of the relationship between anxiety and despair in Kierkegaard is that of Kresten Nordentoft. Nordentoft claims that in *The Concept of Anxiety*, there is a basic difference between chapters 1-2 and chapters 3-4. In chapters 1-2, anxiety is dealt with in relation to hereditary sin. Nordentoft claims that chapters 3 and 4 are a clouded first run through the same material covered later in *The Sickness Unto Death*.

> The difference between the two principal psychological works (*Anxiety* & *Sickness*) is specifically one of terminology and subject area. They are so different in terminology that it is only upon a reflective analysis that one sees that they are dealing with the same problem. . . . The third and fourth chapters of *The Concept of Anxiety* deal with the same questions which are dealt with again, in a more clarified and definitive form, in the entirety of *The Sickness Unto Death* (Nordentoft 1972, xxi).

Nordentoft equates anxiety of the good, which Kierkegaard explains in chapter 4 of *The Concept of Anxiety*, with Kierkegaard's discussion of despair in *The Sickness Unto Death*. Nordentoft is correct in claiming that the third and fourth chapters of *The Concept of Anxiety* are not as clear as *The Sickness Unto Death*, but this is not because the same phenomenon is described more clearly in the later work. Rather, in chapters 3 and 4 of *The Concept of Anxiety*, and particularly in the section titled "Anxiety of the Good," Vigilius is describing the anxiety of someone who is in sin. Vigilius tacitly assumes an understanding of sin as despair before God, a view which is only made explicit in *The Sickness Unto Death*. He is not there describing despair, i.e., the misrelation of the self to itself and to God, but the anxiety of one who is in sin. Hence, Nordentoft is incorrect when he claims the two works describe the same phenomenon. Robert Perkins seems to make the same mistake when he writes "The [anxiety] of the good is despair" (1969, 30).

(3) Many commentators have made no explicit statement on the interrelationship between anxiety and despair but have still tacitly acknowledged an interconnection. This shows itself in the way in which they have organized their work so that anxiety and despair are treated in succession. For example, Calvin Schrag discusses Kierkegaard's conceptions of anxiety and despair in different sections of his chapter titled "Anxiety and Finitude," though he makes no mention of the connection between the two (1961). A similar tactic is used by Mark Taylor in his work *Kierkegaard's Pseudonymous Authorship* (1975), John Elrod in *Being and Existence in Kierkegaard's Pseudonymous Works* (1975), Alistair Hannay in *Kierkegaard* (1982), Louis Dupré in *Kierkegaard as Theologian* (1963), L.L. Miller in *In Search of the Self* (1962), J. Preston Cole in *The Problematic Self in Kierkegaard and Freud* (1971), and C. Stephen Evans in *Søren Kierkegaard's Christian Psychology* (1990). Since the relation between anxiety and despair are not central concerns of these writers, it is not surprising that they do not explicitly explore it. Still, these authors recognize a basic interconnection between anxiety and despair in the thought of Kierkegaard inasmuch as they group the two phenomena together.

(4) A final account of the relationship between anxiety and despair is that of George E. and George B. Arbaugh. They correctly point out that

> *Sickness* is in no sense a revised version of [*The Concept of Anxiety.*] Anxiety as treated in [*The Concept of Anxiety*] is the very mark of humanness, under the responsibility of freedom. Despair, as treated in *Sickness*, is the dreadful sickness that befalls spirit through its wrong use of freedom (1968, 297).

Stephan Dunning presents the same interpretation when he writes "anxiety is only the condition of sin, whereas despair is sin itself" (1985, 216).[6] This view is essentially correct, and certainly an improvement on that of Nordentoft, for Nordentoft mistakenly claims that *The Sickness Unto Death* is a revised version of *The Concept of Anxiety*. However, because these statements by the Arbaughs and by Dunning were written within the context different topics, these authors do not adequately explore in detail the interconnections between anxiety and despair.

Based on the above, it follows that what little work there is on the relationship between the concepts anxiety and despair in Kierkegaard's thought is either incorrect or incomplete.

3. Methods and Procedures

When one faces Kierkegaard's writings, one meets a tremendous number of volumes including several very different styles of writing. Therefore, we must determine which merit the most attention for this topic.

Kierkegaard's writings can be roughly divided into four main groups: (1) pseudonymous works, (2) discourses (edifying and Christian), (3) the journals, and (4) the later writings to which he signed his name. For my purposes, the most important of these are the pseudonymous works, for it is in the pseudonymous works that Kierkegaard most clearly develops the concepts of anxiety and despair along with his view of the self and insights about the meaning of freedom and its misuses.[7] In the discourses, there is some discussion of both anxiety and despair, though Kierkegaard does not provide the conceptual clarification of these terms in the discourses as he does in the pseudonymous works. Likewise, the journals contain entries concerning both anxiety and despair. While these entries sometimes give concrete examples or clear explanations that are helpful, they are at other times too condensed to be illuminating and sometimes cryptic. I will use the discourses and the journals insofar as they help explain the two main works of this study, though I will not be focusing on the discussions of anxiety and despair in the discourses or the journals with the goal of understanding them in themselves. Finally, Kierkegaard's later writings have little immediate bearing on the relationship between anxiety and despair. In them, he is concerned primarily with ecclesial and political issues of 19th century Denmark. There is no later substantive development of the concepts of anxiety or despair in these works. Therefore, the pseudonymous literature, and in particular, *The Concept of Anxiety* and *The Sickness Unto Death*, will be the focus of my work, with the other works being used to help clarify points.

At the end of a century which may well be described as the age of anxiety, in a time marked by debate about the meaning of human freedom, we find ourselves longing to be free. By pressing Kierkegaard so that we might better understand the relationship between anxiety and despair, we seek not only insight into human freedom, but a diagnosis of the ailment whose cure is the freedom that frees.

CHAPTER 2

A Preparatory Examination of Several Topics Related to *The Concept of Anxiety*

Before drawing out Kierkegaard's ideas on freedom and anxiety in *The Concept of Anxiety*, there are several preliminary issues to examine.

1. The Danish Term Angest

While those who write in English on Kierkegaard almost all now use "anxiety" to translate Kierkegaard's term "*angest*," it has not always been that way. (In 19th century Danish, there were two acceptable spellings of the term under consideration: *angest* and *angst*. In contemporary Danish the spelling *angest* is no longer used.)[1] According to Walter Lowrie, in the first translations of passages from Kierkegaard's writings that were published in 1924 by Hollander, the term *angest* was translated as "dread." In Lowrie's 1940 translation of *Stages on Life's Way*, the term *angest* is used eight times with five different translations. His translations include "dread," "anxiety," "anguish," "foreboding," and "agony"(*SLW*, 109, 203, 228, 240, 289). These are not the only words that have been used to translate *angest* into English. Douglas Steere, the translator of *Purity of Heart* translates *angest* once as "afraid" (*PH*, 167). David Swenson, the translator of *The Gospel of Suffering*, twice translates *angest* as "fear"

(*GS*, 38 & 86.). Despite these various translations, Lowrie claimed in the preface to his 1943 translation of *Begrebet Angest* that everyone had agreed to use the term dread "after a desperate search for something better" (*CDread*, x). Lowrie explains his decision to use the term "dread" in the first complete English translation of *Begrebet Angest* by claiming that the French translators, who had used *angoisse*, did not capture the proper connotation, that is, that *angest* "is an apprehension of the future, a presentiment of a something which is 'nothing'" (*CDread*, x). Lowrie does not mention the term "anxiety" as an alternative, though he himself had already used anxiety as a translation of *angest* in other works (*SLW*, 109 & 240).

The problem is further complicated by several factors. There are other Danish terms that are close to the English term "anxiety" in meaning. Further, Lowrie had already used "anxiety" to translate *bekymring* in his 1941 translation of the *Christian Discourses*. In the *Christian Discourses*, *bekymring* has the meaning "inordinate worry about something that is not in one's control" as in the exhortation "do not worry," or "be not afraid," though in different contexts *bekymring* can also mean "care" or "concern."[2] Kierkegaard also uses the term *angest* in the *Christian Discourses*, but it refers to one's relationship to the future and is translated by Lowrie as "dread" (though the first time the term appears he translates it as "anguishing dread" and notes that he is dissatisfied with the translation). There is a third Danish term that comes close to the English term "anxiety" in meaning: *plage*. *Plage* is etymologically related to the English term "plague," and can mean "to worry or to trouble," though its connotation is often stronger when it means "to torment." In the *Christian Discourses*, Lowrie translates *plage* as "worry." The Danish term *selvplagelsens* can also mean "inordinate worry," though it is well translated by Lowrie as "self-torment." Hence, there are at least four Danish terms that

Kierkegaard uses that could be translated as "anxiety." It would probably be best if each of these Danish terms is translated by a different English term in order to make it clear to readers of English that Kierkegaard is using different terms.[3]

"Anxiety" was the term chosen to translate *angest* in Reidar Thomte's 1980 retranslation of *Begrebet Angest*, though this was not without precedence. David Swenson rather consistently translated *angst* as anxiety in his 1944 translation of *Either/Or*. Also, the Hongs had used "anxiety" in their translations of the *Journals*.

There are several solid reasons for preferring the term "anxiety" to "dread." "Anxiety" is etymologically closer to the Danish than is "dread." In English, "dread" generally has the connotation of fear of something; it would be odd for an English speaker to express dread of "nothing" whereas it is not so odd to be anxious about nothing. Moreover, "anxiety" is the term used to translate Heidegger's term *angst*. Since there is an affinity between the way the two use the term, as there is with Jaspers, Tillich, Rollo May, and others, it is sensible to use the same English term for all: "anxiety."

Some have suggested using the term "angst" rather than "anxiety" or "dread," but this solution has several shortcomings. First, this is a transliteration, not a translation of the term. Also, it may give the wrong connotation, that is, that Kierkegaard is using a technical term of European existentialism. He is not. Rather, he is using a common word in the Danish language and giving it a very precise, perhaps technical, meaning. Since anxiety is a common word in English, but one capable of being refined in meaning, it is preferable to angst.

Mark Taylor has preferred using the term "dread," claiming "anxiety" "is not a strong enough word to express the terrifying aspect of the experience that Kierkegaard is discussing" (1975, 219). But to accent the terrifying is to miss a crucial part of the concept. *Angest* is both an attraction to and a repulsion from the nothingness of future possibilities. "Anxiety" seems to capture the crucial tension between eagerness and uneasiness in Kierkegaard's concept more completely than does dread. Therefore, I will follow Hong and Thomte in using the term "anxiety."

Finally, it is important to note that Kierkegaard has two distinct but related meanings of the term "anxiety." Further, he does not always make it clear in which sense he is using the term, and sometimes he seems to be using the term in both senses. The concept of anxiety is important for Kierkegaard not simply because he is interested in describing and probing human emotions, but because he is seeking insight into being human. To be sure, anxiety is a felt affect, but Kierkegaard does not limit his discussion of anxiety to the feeling or mood of anxiety. Rather, he goes on to describe the structure of the human self, of which anxiety gives us insight. In places, Kierkegaard goes so far in the direction of equating anxiety and the corresponding structure of human being that it is evident that he has not restricted his use of the term "anxiety" to the domain of feelings. For example, he writes that spirit relates itself to itself as anxiety (*CA*, 44). But to call the relation of spirit to itself anxiety is to speak of anxiety as a structure of human being, that is, as an ontological structure. Therefore, Kierkegaard sometimes uses the term "anxiety" to refer to a feeling or range of feelings, sometimes to refer to the structure of human being that gives rise to that feeling, sometimes both, and often he is ambiguous as to whether a particular use of the term is meant to denote a feeling, a structure of human existence, or both.

2. The Concept of Anxiety in Other Writings by Kierkegaard

As one would expect, Kierkegaard discusses and explains the concept of anxiety more in *The Concept of Anxiety* than in any other of his writings. Still, he employs the term in other works, and hence these merit some attention.[4] The use of the concept of anxiety in Kierkegaard's writings other than *The Concept of Anxiety* can be divided into two groups: those uses of the term in which there is some explanation and clarification of the concept and those in which there is none. For example, though Kierkegaard used the term *angest* twice in his dissertation *The Concept of Irony*, he does not explain or define the term. While I have listed the works in which all of the uses of the term *angest* appear (see the preceding note), only those that include an explanation of the term merit attention.

Kierkegaard's first explanation of the concept of anxiety in a published work appears in *Either/Or* Vol. 1, in the essay titled "The Ancient Tragical Motive as Reflected in the Modern." There, "A" is distinguishing between the Greek notion of tragedy and its modern correlate. In this context, he describes anxiety as a category of modern tragedy distinct from the Greek notion of tragedy and essentially different from sorrow. "Anxiety is the means by which the subject appropriates his sorrow and assimilates it," though while anxiety is attracted to sorrow as a lover to his beloved, it has a double relation to its object as "it both loves and fears it" (*E/O* I, L152, H154-55). A similar explanation of the term appears in an 1842 journal entry where Kierkegaard writes:

> Anxiety is a desire for what one fears, a sympathetic antipathy; anxiety is an alien power which grips the individual, and yet one cannot tear himself free from it and does not want to, for one fears, but what he fears he desires (*SKJP* I, 94)

In these passages, the tension of anxiety, the simultaneous attraction and repulsion, is made clear, though there is no explanation of the object of anxiety.

The first clear focus on the object of anxiety comes in an 1844 journal entry when he writes: "It is quite possible to show that a very precise and correct usage of language links anxiety and the future together. . . . Thus far one easily sees that the future and the possible correspond to it" (*SKJP* I, 98). While this connection is made clear in *The Concept of Anxiety*, it is probably most explicit in the *Christian Discourses* in which Kierkegaard bluntly states "What is anxiety? It is the next day" (*CDisc*, 80). Anxiety differs from fear in that one fears a specific object, whereas anxiety has no specific object in the present.

Those familiar with Heidegger may be surprised by how little Kierkegaard writes about the anxiety of death. For Kierkegaard anxiety's object is any future possibility. Of course, this includes death. Kierkegaard speaks specifically of the anxiety of death in *Purity of Heart*, where he describes how one can be attracted to one's own destruction. (*PH*, 65). He describes the anxiety of death again in *The Gospel of Suffering* (*GS*, 86). Closely related to this description is the description of looking into an abyss and desiring to plunge oneself in while yet being repulsed from the thought (*PH*, 65). Hence, for Kierkegaard, anxiety's object can be any future possibility, including one's own death.

In many of Kierkegaard's other works, when he employs the term "anxiety," he does little to explain the technical meaning he attaches to it. Often the word seems to refer only to worry. For example, the first *Edifying Discourse* begins with a prayer which includes the line "We take with us the memory of fearful doubts which were set at rest, of anxieties which were solaced, of the downcast mind which was cheered and strengthened" (*ED* I, 6). In such uses, Kierkegaard does not appear to be employing the term in the technical sense that he developed and made explicit in *The Concept of Anxiety*. This is true of his use of the term in *Fear and Trembling*, though he does briefly discuss the concept of anxiety in relation to the story of Abraham. Rejecting previous treatments of the story of Abraham, he writes "What is omitted from Abraham's story is anxiety" (*FT*, 28). However, there is little or no clarification of the concept of anxiety and its relation to Abraham in *Fear and Trembling*.

In a number of works written later than *The Concept of Anxiety*, the term "anxiety" is used, but with direct reference to *The Concept of Anxiety*.[5] In such places, no new development of the concept occurs. However, there are several later journal entries in which Kierkegaard appeared to be developing the concept further than he did in *The Concept of Anxiety*. For example, in an 1847 entry Kierkegaard wrote:

> Deep within every human being there still lives the anxiety over the possibility of being alone in the world, forgotten by God, overlooked among the millions and millions in this enormous household. One keeps this anxiety at a distance by looking at the many round about who are related to him as kin and friends, but the anxiety is still there (*SKJP* I, 100).

This kind of anxiety, of being alone while in a crowd, is not developed in *The Concept of Anxiety*, though neither is it significantly different structurally from the types of anxiety described in *The Concept of Anxiety*, since it refers to one's ambiguous relation to a future possibility. Moreover, this theme of being alone in a crowd was surely much on Kierkegaard's mind in 1847 (three years after he had written *The Concept of Anxiety*), as this is one of the main themes of *Purity of Heart*, which was written in that year. In 1850, another entry appears in Kierkegaard's journals that may indicate an attempt to develop the concept of anxiety beyond what he had written in *The Concept of Anxiety*. The entry reads simply: "Anxiety is actually nothing but impatience" (*SKJP* I, 103). However, Kierkegaard never further developed the thought, so it is unclear if this is to be a different or additional aspect of the concept of anxiety, or if it was simply a thought he recorded, perhaps to develop later, but unable to do so in the last four years of his short life.

3. The Pseudonym: Vigilius Haufniensis

As Louis Mackey has pointed out, Kierkegaard's work needs to be analyzed not only as pure philosophy or theology, but also with the tools of literary criticism (1971). Hence, it is in order to begin with questions that concern more the literary form and presentation of the works than the philosophical content. Since *The Concept of Anxiety* is a pseudonymous work, a thorough examination of the work will include, or even begin with, an examination of the pseudonym "Vigilius Haufniensis."

While much has been made of the significance of Kierkegaard's pseudonyms, there has been very little written about Vigilius Haufniensis, either by commentators or by Kierkegaard himself. In *The Point of View for My Work as an Author*, Kierkegaard argues at length that the purpose of the aesthetic literature (i.e., the pseudonymous works published between 1843-46 including *Either/Or, Repetition, Fear and Trembling, Philosophical Fragments, The Concept of Anxiety, Stages on Life's Way*, and *The Concluding Unscientific Postscript*) is to provide an aesthetic counterpart to the religious, upbuilding (edifying) literature,[6] but one that points to the religious. However, *The Concept of Anxiety* is only briefly mentioned in a footnote as part of a list of aesthetic works. While some of the other works are discussed and explained, *The Concept of Anxiety* receives no further mention. In what sense is *The Concept of Anxiety* to be classed along with the rest of the aesthetic literature? And in what sense is the pseudonymity of this work different from the rest of the pseudonymous literature?

About half way through *The Concluding Unscientific Postscript*, Climacus includes an Appendix entitled "A Glance at a Contemporary Effort in Danish Literature." Here, each of the pseudonymous works is briefly reviewed. Climacus writes "*The Concept of Anxiety* differs essentially from the other pseudonymous writings in having a direct form, and in being even a little bit objectively dogmatic" (*CUP*, L241, H I 269-70). This signifies that Kierkegaard saw Vigilius Haufniensis as essentially different from the other aesthetic pseudonyms.

This passage from the *Postscript* goes on to state that along with *The Concept of Anxiety* "there came simultaneously a merry little book by Nicholaus Notabene" (*CUP*, L241, H I 270). By this, Climacus refers to *Prefaces* which was published on June 17, 1844, the same day that *The Concept of Anxiety* was. *Prefaces* is a humorous work. Nicholaus Notabene, the pseudonymous author, is forbidden by his wife to write a book. Hence, he limits himself to writing the prefaces to books. The humor of the work is significant inasmuch as *The Concept of Anxiety* is not accompanied by an upbuilding discourse, as were all of Kierkegaard's previous pseudonymous works. Since Kierkegaard considered *The Concept of Anxiety* to be of such a serious nature, he accompanied it with a humorous work rather than an upbuilding discourse. Hence, in the case of *The Concept of Anxiety*, the balance between the aesthetic literature and the more serious, religious, upbuilding discourses is changed. This gives us further evidence that Kierkegaard viewed *The Concept of Anxiety* as essentially different from the other pseudonymous works that comprise the aesthetic literature.

The end of the *Concluding Unscientific Postscript* includes "A First and Last Declaration" signed by Kierkegaard. In it he admits he produced all of the pseudonymous works though he denies that they represent his views. He writes:

> In the pseudonymous works there is not a single word
> which is mine, I have no opinion about these works ex-
> cept as a third person, no knowledge of their meaning
> except as a reader, not the remotest private relation to
> them, since such a thing is impossible in the case of a
> doubly reflected communication (*CUP*, L551, H I 626).

Walter Lowrie has suggested that we disregard the admonition and consider "everything we find in it to be safely
regarded as [Kierkegaard's] own way of thinking" (*CDread*,
x). Lowrie's interpretation seems to make the pseudonym
superfluous. Our goal will be to understand three things:
why Kierkegaard used a pseudonym, the character of this
pseudonym, and the difference between this pseudonym
and those of other early pseudonymous works, especially
Either/Or and *The Stages on Life's Way*.

There is very little mention of Vigilius Haufniensis in
Kierkegaard's journals. This is notably different from some
of the other pseudonyms, which are discussed and explained in greater detail in the journals. However, from
his journals, we learn that Kierkegaard had planned to
sign his own name to this, his first direct work since his
dissertation (*Pap.* VB 42 n.d. 1844). Moreover, besides
writing out a title page with his name on it, he had gone
so far as to write a preface appropriate to his signing the
book. (After he changed his mind and decided to use a
pseudonym, he did not discard his preface. Instead he
used it as No. VII in the above mentioned *Prefaces*.)

His decision to use a pseudonym did not keep him
from dedicating the work to P.M. Møller, his favorite
teacher. As both Lowrie and Thomte point out, this is
evidence that *The Concept of Anxiety* is not strictly anony-
mous, even though Kierkegaard discarded several phrases
from the dedication which were more strongly personal
(*CDread*, x; *CA*, 223).

Walter Lowrie speculates that the reason Kierkegaard
decided to make the work pseudonymous is "perhaps

because it contained so intimate a confession of his 'stern upbringing from innate dread to faith.'" Hence, Kierkegaard "hid behind the name Vigilius Haufniensis" (*CDread*, x). This may be correct, but it seems implausible since the dedication nearly amounts to an announcement that Kierkegaard is responsible for writing the book. Instead, there is another reason why Kierkegaard did not sign the work. One of the few entries in the *Journals* on Vigilius Haufniensis reads:

> Some people may be disturbed by my sketch of an observer in *The Concept of Anxiety*. It does, however, belong there and is like a watermark in the work. After all, I always have a poetic relationship to my works, and therefore I am pseudonymous. At the same time as the book develops some theme, the corresponding individuality is delineated. For example, Vigilius Haufniensis delineates several, but I have also made a sketch of him in the book (*SKJP* V, 5732).

However, the sketch of Vigilius in the book is not strong. There is only a very brief explicit description of Vigilius in *The Concept of Anxiety*. Moreover, his personality traits do not overtly exhibit themselves in the writing. There are, however, enough clues to piece together a character sketch of Vigilius Haufniensis.

The name "Vigilius Haufniensis" literally means "watchman of the harbor," that is, of Copenhagen, a harbor town. In the preface, Vigilius insists that the Latinate form of his name is not meant to be pretentious. He supplies the Danish name "Christen Madsen," an ordinary name, in its stead. He writes: "Nothing could please me more than to be regarded as a layman who indeed speculates but is still far removed from speculation" (*CA*, 8). A related journal entry reads "Most of all I wish to be regarded as an alehouse keeper, innkeeper, or as a plain layman who walks the floor and speculates without wishing that his speculative result should be regarded as speculation" (*Pap.* V B 72:5 n.d., 1844).

Thus, just as Kierkegaard denied that he wrote with
authority in the prefaces of his upbuilding discourses,
Vigilius makes it clear that he is just an ordinary layman
who speculates. He does not write with the official authority decreed by the church. When he claims that his
speculative result should not be regarded as speculation,
he means to deny that he has the pomp and certitude
associated with the caricatured Hegelian philosopher.

There is virtually nothing more in *The Concept of Anxiety* that provides us explicit information about this pseudonym. The introduction gives us further insight into the
character of Vigilius, but only if we look for implied char-
acteristics. The main point in the introduction is analogous to the point that Aristotle makes in the *Nichomachean
Ethics*, when he states that each area of study must be
proportioned to that which it studies. One cannot study
ethics in the same way that one studies mathematics.[7]
Analogously, Kierkegaard claims that one cannot study
psychology in the same way that one studies dogmatics.
The polemic against Hegel in the introduction is primarily for pedagogical, not philosophical purposes. Hegel is
being used as an example of how not to proceed in approaching the study of a subject. Vigilius claims he will
not confuse psychology with dogmatics the way that Hegel
confused logic with ethics. Thus we learn that Vigilius,
though one who speculates, is at pains not to conflate the
study of one subject into a domain not properly proportioned to it.

One might also ask what existential sphere Vigilius
occupies. Kierkegaard's works present his famous view
of the dialectical development of spirit from the aesthetic
sphere where one lives for pleasure, to the ethical sphere
where one lives for duty, and finally to the religious sphere,
where faith is paramount. In what existential sphere is
Vigilius? While it is true that Kierkegaard refers to *The
Concept of Anxiety* as an aesthetic work, he does so only

when discussing the entire group of pseudonymous works that he wrote before the *Postscript* (*PV*, 16). If we remember that he has had Climacus admit that *The Concept of Anxiety* is essentially different from the other early pseudonymous works "in having a direct form, and in being a little bit objectively dogmatic," (*CUP*, L241, H I 269-70), it is reasonable to assume that just because Kierkegaard groups *The Concept of Anxiety* with the other early pseudonymous works, that does not imply that the pseudonymous author is an aesthete who lives solely for pleasure.

One may be tempted to claim that Vigilius occupies the ethical sphere. Mark Taylor may be implying this when he discusses "Dreadfulness" as a section in a chapter entitled "The Ethical Stage of Existence" (1975). But we will see that anxiety pervades all three spheres. Moreover, I will offer a reason why Vigilius should be considered, at least partially, as a religious writer.

All of Kierkegaard's religious writings include two important categories: earnestness and an upbuilding quality. This is made clear in the preface to *The Sickness Unto Death*, which is indisputably a Christian, religious work in Kierkegaard's view. There, Anti-Climacus writes: "Everything essentially Christian must have in its presentation a resemblance to the way a physician speaks at the sick bed," that is, in earnest (*SUD*, 5). By "earnestness," Kierkegaard means an existential response to the awareness that one is a sinner. Vigilius discusses earnestness in some detail in *The Concept of Anxiety* (*CA*, 15-6, 147-50). He goes so far as to write that "corresponding to the concept of sin is earnestness" (*CA*, 15). Hence, though Vigilius the watchman may be an observer, he is not a detached observer. His earnestness is not of the same quality as that of Johannes Climacus. It was not lack of earnestness in the work that kept Kierkegaard's name from the title page. More likely, it was because the work does not explicitly have an upbuilding quality to it.

The second feature of Kierkegaard's religious literature is that it includes an upbuilding quality. Again, in the
preface to *The Sickness Unto Death*, Anti-Climacus writes
"From the Christian point of view, everything, indeed
everything, ought to serve for upbuilding" (*SUD*, 6). It is
on this point that *The Concept of Anxiety* differs from
Kierkegaard's religious literature to which he signs his
name. Is *The Concept of Anxiety* essentially upbuilding?
Here we must proceed with caution. While *The Sickness
Unto Death* is subtitled "A Christian Exposition for
Upbuilding and Awakening," *The Concept of Anxiety* is
subtitled "A Simple Psychologically Orienting Deliberation on the Dogmatic Issue of Hereditary Sin." Moreover,
the content of Sickness is aimed more clearly at edification, while *The Concept of Anxiety* is an educative deliberation. Hence, *The Sickness Unto Death* has more of the
character of a Christian, religious writing in Kierkegaard's
authorship than does *The Concept of Anxiety*.

It is important to note, though, that this difference
does not imply a lack of Christianity in Vigilius Haufniensis.
It does not follow that if Vigilius's book is not upbuilding,
he is not a Christian. Rather, the reason that Vigilius's
book is an educative deliberation rather than an upbuilding
exposition lies in the immediate goal of the book, not in
the character of its pseudonymous author. Since the concept of anxiety had not been adequately clarified before
the writing of the book, its use in an upbuilding discourse
would be incomplete. Further, in his introduction, Vigilius
makes it clear that anxiety is properly understood within
the domain of psychology and without reference to dogmatics. Yet, anxiety is related to dogmatics inasmuch as it
is the condition for the possibility of actual sin. Vigilius is
aware that books about actual sin properly have the purpose of upbuilding, for as he points out, sin does not
belong in any science, but rather is properly the subject
of the sermon (*CA*, 16). Hence, the immediate goal of *The*

Concept of Anxiety is to clarify the meaning of anxiety; this conceptual clarification points directly to dogmatics insofar as anxiety is the condition for the possibility of actual sin. A discussion of actual sin, however, lies outside of the scope of the book.

One may ask why Vigilius would write about something other than that which would have an upbuilding character. The answer is simply that *The Concept of Anxiety* hopes to answer questions raised by Christianity. The purpose, then, of *The Concept of Anxiety* is to be an educative deliberation that answers questions raised by Christianity, but not to deal with precisely Christian issues - dogmatics - for that would entail methodological confusion. *The Concept of Anxiety* uses a psychological method, that is, it makes no reference to teachings available only through revelation.[8]

We are now able to answer a number of questions raised about the pseudonym Vigilius Haufniensis. As to why Kierkegaard decided to use the pseudonym, "thin" as it may be, rather than sign his own name to the work, the most cogent reason seems to be that the work does not have the edifying or upbuilding nature of the other early works to which he signed his name. Vigilius is a Christian layman who "speculates" about the human self in the context of Danish Lutheranism. His speculation points in the direction of dogmatics, but it is not dogmatic since its subject matter lies in the domain of psychology, not dogmatics. While his deliberation is not upbuilding by itself, it both points to that which is upbuilding and answers questions that may arise in the context of Christianity. These are not the questions of a disinterested observer, but the questions of an earnest Christian: what must a human be such that he is capable both of sinning and of redemption?

In his introduction, Vigilius writes:

> The present work has set as its task the psychological treatment of the concept of "anxiety," but in such a way that it constantly keeps *in mente* and before its eye the dogma of hereditary sin. Accordingly, it must also, although tacitly so, deal with the concept of sin (*CA*, 21).

Hence, *The Concept of Anxiety* is a book written by an author in earnestness which, though not of an explicitly upbuilding nature itself, seeks to be a psychologically orienting deliberation on an issue raised by Christianity.

In *The Point of View For My Work as an Author*, Kierkegaard maintains that all of the aesthetic works serve to prepare the reader for the religious sphere of existence and specifically for Christianity. Hence, even though its form is direct and its author is earnest, *The Concept of Anxiety* may be classed among the other early pseudonymous works as aesthetic. The aesthetic literature, then, does not necessarily refer to works by authors who are aesthetes, nor to any flaw in the author's perspective. Rather, the aesthetic literature is comprised of works that prepare and point the way to religiousness but that are not themselves explicitly upbuilding. Hence, it is possible that while Vigilius Haufniensis is at the religious level, he has written an aesthetic work. The pseudonymity of the work is due to the fact that the immediate goal of the book does not include edification; the pseudonymity is not due to the pseudonym's character.

The Concept of Anxiety is different from the other aesthetic works primarily in that it is explicitly educative. It seeks to clarify a concept which is crucial for understanding human being and the Christian notions of sin and original sin. The other aesthetic works, most notably *Either/Or* and *Stages on Life's Way*, are indirect. They are indirect in that Kierkegaard is not directly communicating his views to the reader, but presenting views that others would hold by developing characters who would existentially adopt such views. Instead of explaining crucial concepts, these works present characters and record their particular, individual experiences of being human. The indirect works are not aimed primarily at accounting for or explaining the experiences. Their aim is to show rather than to tell. *The Concept of Anxiety* differs from these works in that it, as Climacus tells us, "has a direct form" (*CUP*, L241, H I 269). Therefore, there must be something other than "indirectness" that *The Concept of Anxiety* shares with the other aesthetic works to be grouped together with them. The answer is this. The indirect works are similar to *The Concept of Anxiety* in that they prepare the reader for and point to religiousness and Christianity without themselves being upbuilding. Yet, *The Concept of Anxiety* is quite different from the rest of the other aesthetic works in that its form is that of a direct educative deliberation.

Vigilius Haufniensis is a Christian layman who speculates about questions raised by Christianity. His writing is direct and earnest. The work almost has the style of a dissertation. In this way, the work is quite different from the other early pseudonymous works. Vigilius's speculation is not the grandiose philosophizing of a Hegelian. Rather, he hopes to deliberate earnestly on questions raised by Christianity.

4. *The Phenomenological Method in* The Concept of Anxiety

Vigilius does not describe his method in *The Concept of Anxiety* as phenomenological, though it is not unreasonable to do so. For example, Vincent McCarthy has written of the "phenomenology of moods" in Kierkegaard (1978). If, like McCarthy, we take phenomenology to mean the use of self-reflection and analysis in order to achieve a descriptive study of a given subject matter, then Kierkegaard's method is, at least in part, phenomenological.

In explaining his method, Vigilius criticizes the method of taking a detached stance while attempting to observe these phenomena in others, as in empirical psychology. There are three main faults with the attempt to understand anxiety and sin through the observation of the behavior of others. First, anxiety and sin are only known in their completeness when one experiences them. Vigilius writes: "How sin came into the world, each man understands solely by himself. If he would learn it from another, he would *eo ipso* misunderstand it" (*CA*, 51). Sin can be understood only inasmuch as it is one's own sin. Second, one's own affections and psychological states are always present at hand. Therefore, descriptions of them will be more rich and less diluted than descriptions of another's affects. One traditional means of acquiring examples for psychological analysis was through characters from literature. Vigilius criticizes this method along with the methods of empirical psychology; instead, the psychologist should duplicate the affect himself. Then "he will have no need to take his examples from literary repertoires and serve up half-dead reminiscences, but will bring his observations entirely fresh from the water, wriggling and sparkling in the play of their colors" (*CA*, 55). Finally, empirical psychology's attempt to understand being human through the observation of the behavior of others leads to another undesirable consequence: it forces the psychologist to go on a senseless search for people to observe who are experiencing this or that affect. Using Kierkegaard's phenomenological method of self-reflection, one will not "have to run himself to death to become aware of something" (*CA*, 55).

Instead, the phenomenological method that Vigilius employs consists of duplicating affects and psychological states oneself and using that as material for description and analysis. Vigilius writes:

> One who has properly occupied himself with psychology and psychological observation acquires a general human flexibility that enables him at once to construct his example which even though it lacks factual authority nevertheless has an authority of a different kind. The psychological observer ought to be more nimble than a tightrope dancer in order to incline and bend himself to other people and imitate their attitudes, and his silence in the moment of confidence should be seductive and voluptuous, so that what is hidden may find satisfaction in slipping out to chat with itself in the artificially constructed nonobservance and silence. Hence he ought also to have a poetic originality in his soul so as to create both the totality and the invariable from what in the individual is always partially and variably present. . . . [W]hat he needs he has at hand at once by virtue of his general practice, just as in a well-equipped house one need not carry in water from the street but has it on his level by high pressure. . . . His observation will have the quality of freshness and the interest of actuality if he is prudent enough to control his observations. To that end he imitates in himself every mood, every psychic state that he discovers in another (*CA*, 54-5).

This method of duplicating moods and psychological states and then using one's subjective experiences as material for philosophical reflection is based on the principle *unum noris omnes* (if you know one, you know all) (*CA*, 79). That part of human being that is common to all humans is available through self-reflection. Vigilius is here examining anxiety and sin. These phenomena cannot be satisfactorily studied by the observation of the behaviors of others. Instead, Vigilius employs the method of phenomenological self-reflection in order that through self-knowledge of what is common to all, he may acquire a deeper understanding of human being. For, as Vigilius writes, "this is the wonder of life, that each man who is mindful of himself knows what no science knows, since he knows who he himself is" (*CA*, 78-9).

With this background, we can begin to draw out the themes of freedom and anxiety through a reading of *The Concept of Anxiety*.

CHAPTER 3

Anxiety in
The Concept of Anxiety

1. The Introduction:
Psychology and Dogmatics

In the introduction to *The Concept of Anxiety*, Vigilius
Haufniensis sets forth and defends both the goal and
the method of the book. The goal of the book is to
provide a "psychological treatment of the concept of
'anxiety,'" in order to gain a better understanding of the
dogmatic concept of original sin (*CA*, 14). For us to make
sense of the introduction, we must understand what
Vigilius takes to be the domains of psychology and of
dogmatics, as well as why the two are distinct and yet
related.

After a subtitle that makes it clear that the goal of the
introduction is to make explicit both the distinction and
relation between psychology and dogmatics, the text of
the introduction begins with a polemic against Hegel.
Kierkegaard is not here criticizing merely for sport. Rather,
he uses his criticism of Hegel to explain the distinction
between psychology and dogmatics. According to Vigilius,
Hegel did not always adequately limit his method of study
to the topic or subject matter for which that particular
method is proper. For example, Hegel confused logic,

the study of the necessary, with actuality, which is
contingent.[1] Likewise, when faith is explained in the terms
of logic, it entails confusing methods proper to distinct
subjects. For example, it is only by an equivocation and a
misconstrual of method that one can use the term "reconciliation" or "atonement" both in logic and in dogmatics.
Vigilius's charge against Hegel is that in attempting to
arrive at a system, he sometimes confused the method-
ologies of essentially different subject matters. He sometimes used a method appropriate for one subject in order
to understand a different one. This confusion in method
inevitably leads to flawed conclusions. Therefore, Vigilius
insists that he must properly locate the subject of his study
in its proper domain and use only the method of study
that is appropriate to that domain.

The subject of the study is anxiety. Anxiety, since it is
a phenomenon essential to human beings, is studied by
psychology. By psychology, Kierkegaard does not mean
empirical psychology in the contemporary sense. Rather,
he uses the term "psychology" in the classical sense to
mean the study, description, and explanation of the human soul, or of the human being and that which is essential to being human.[2] Perhaps the contemporary term
"philosophical anthropology" is closest to what Vigilius
means by "psychology." While the specific method of
Vigilius's psychology is different from the method of most
philosophical anthropologists,[3] there is an essential similarity between the two: both use a method which is available to all humans through the use of experience and
imagination. One need not appeal to divine revelation
nor have religious presuppositions in order to use Vigilius's
psychological methodology.

Nonetheless, Vigilius is not studying anxiety solely to
acquire increased cognitive understanding of being human. He is quite explicit that it is through an understanding of anxiety that we arrive at a better understanding of

sin, and specifically of hereditary sin. However, the method of studying sin is different from the method of studying anxiety since sin is a dogmatic concept. Since dogmatic concepts are based on revelation rather than solely on human experience, the method of studying them must take this into account. If sin were to be taken as something other than a dogmatic concept, for example, if it were studied with the methods of metaphysics or philosophical anthropology, then it would necessarily be misconstrued (*CA*, 14-6). The point is not only that sin should be studied in a dogmatic treatise, but that sin is a topic that concerns the individual and should be dealt with earnestly. Sin requires not only cognitive understanding of the self, but more importantly, an existential response. The proper stance for the discussion of sin is earnestness, and the proper place to discuss sin is in the sermon. Hence, Vigilius writes: "Sin does not properly belong in any science, but it is the subject of the sermon, in which the single individual speaks as the single individual to the single individual" (*CA*, 16). This is not because the concept of sin cannot be grasped cognitively at all, but because sin is primarily a religious, existential category. Since Vigilius insists that *The Concept of Anxiety* is not a dogmatic work (as it uses the methods of "psychology,") and because sin is a dogmatic concept, he includes very little explicit discussion of sin in the work. As we will see,[4] this leads to a difficulty, since Vigilius repeatedly uses the concept of sin without ever adequately explaining his understanding of it.

The next point in the introduction is that a study of ethics cannot shed light on an understanding of sin or original sin (*CA*, 16-23). Vigilius distinguishes two kinds of ethics. The first kind of ethics is naive regarding sin. Making no reference to revelation, it provides an ideal to which we must strive. The first kind of ethics does not concern itself with the fact that people fall short of the ideal. All that it can do is demand that the individual try harder. Therefore, it is unable to explain sin. The second kind of ethics assumes the dogmatic understanding of sin. Its task is to take sinners and make them ethical. However, the second kind of ethics cannot explain sin, since it has simply assumed the dogmatic understanding of sin. It proceeds in virtue of that assumption, but is nonetheless unable to explain what it assumes. Consequently, a study of ethics cannot shed light on an understanding of sin.

The final point in the introduction regards the limits of the psychological study of anxiety and its relation to the concepts of sin and hereditary sin (*CA*, 21-24). A psychological deliberation on the concept of anxiety can shed light on the dogmatic issue of hereditary sin. Psychology, as Haufniensis understands it, is capable of studying human states as long as there is constancy in the state being studied. However, when there is an unwarranted and essential change in the structure of the individual, that is, when the individual acts freely, psychology is unable to explain that act. Psychology can describe the state that precedes such an act. Therefore, psychology can describe the state of the individual prior to sin, namely, anxiety, and the condition for the possibility of sin in humans. It cannot provide a causal explanation of individual sins, however.[5]

Vigilius also uses an implicit distinction between two types of explanations, transcendental explanations, that explain the condition for the possibility of a phenomenon, and causal explanations, that explain the sufficient conditions for a phenomenon. A psychological study of anxiety can shed light on the dogmatic issue of hereditary sin, but psychology is unable to give a causal explanation of sin. This is not due to any deficiency of psychology, but because it is impossible to give a causal explanation of a free act. It is possible to give a transcendental explanation of sin. The state that is the condition for the possibility of sin is a necessary but not a sufficient condition for sin.[6] It is only in this sense, as a description of the condition for the possibility of sin, that *The Concept of Anxiety* is an attempt to explain sin and hereditary sin.

To summarize: in the introduction Vigilius makes it clear that psychology and dogmatics are separate domains and have distinct methods. Psychology, through the use of reason, experience and imagination, is able to describe and explain human states of constancy. Dogmatics asserts by revelation the concept of sin. Psychology is unable to give a causal explanation of individual sins because they are free acts. It is able to describe the state of the individual prior to such free acts. A psychological study of anxiety (the state of the individual before such free acts) will shed light on the dogmatic concept of original sin.

2. Anxiety as the Presupposition of Hereditary Sin

Chapter one begins with a review of the various teachings and explanations of original sin and a rejection of them all.[7] Vigilius's criticism of these accounts of the origin of evil in human beings is not primarily based on sectarian theological grounds. His main rejection rests on the claim that the origin of evil is essentially similar in all human beings. The fundamental mistake in the various interpretations of the Christian dogma of hereditary sin has been to make Adam into someone who stands outside the human race. This has been done in three main ways (*CA*, 25-7). In Catholicism, Adam is placed outside human history by regarding him as being in a state essentially different from the (fallen) human state. In so doing, Adam is made to be essentially different from every other human, since having a history is essential to being human

(*CA*, 25). In the federal theology, Adam acts as a plenipo-
tentiary for the human race. This, too, would make Adam
essentially different from all other humans, and hence
would make Adam not human (*CA*, 25). Others treat the
concept of hereditary sin as if it were essentially different
from sin. On this view, everyone except Adam is a victim
of hereditary sin. But this view is inadequate because it
makes Adam's sin essentially different from that of all
other humans. Also, if Adam's sin, the original sin, is essentially different from every other sin, and if Christ's res-
urrection offers redemption from the effects of original
sin, then Adam is ineligible for redemption (*CA*, 28). Therefore, Vigilius's criticisms of all prior explanations of hereditary sin are based on his view that Adam is a member
of the human race and that no human being can be essentially different from any other human being in regard
to the origin of evil.

    Here, Vigilius sets forth a view of the individual's re-
lation to the rest of the human race that is really different
from the strong "individualism" usually associated with
Kierkegaard. Vigilius writes:

> Each individual has the same perfection, and precisely
> because of this individuals do not fall apart from one
> another numerically any more than the concept of race is
> a phantom. Every individual is essentially interested in
> the history of all other individuals, and just as essentially
> as in his own. Perfection in oneself is therefore the perfect
> participation in the whole (*CA*, 29).

Every human being is essentially similar to every other.
Adam is a human being. Therefore, if the story of Adam is
used to explain hereditary sin, whatever is true of Adam
must be true of every other human being. This is the crux
of Vigilius's rejection of all prior explanations of hereditary sin. Adam "is not essentially different from the race,
for in that case there is no race at all; he is not the race,
for in that case also there would be no race. He is himself
and the race. Therefore that which explains Adam also

explains the race and vice versa" (*CA*, 29). One question that may arise when one reads the first chapter of *The Concept of Anxiety*, especially after having read its introduction, is "Why does Vigilius spend so much ink discussing a dogmatic concept if this is a psychological work?" The problem arises when we erroneously assume that the first chapter is a philosophical/psychological exposition of a dogmatic concept.[8] If that is assumed, then either we ignore Vigilius's introduction or we assume that Vigilius ignored his own introduction. Neither is satisfactory. Hence, in order to preserve the introduction, the first chapter cannot be a philosophical exposition of a dogmatic concept. If it were, it would entail confusing the methods of two domains of study that Vigilius insisted in the introduction must be kept separate.

This apparent problem of interpretation is overcome if we note the similarity between Vigilius's project and that of Kant in his *Religion Within the Limits of Reason Alone*.[9] In Book I of the *Religion*, Kant discussed the radical evil in human nature. In the fourth and final chapter of Book I, Kant examines the origin of evil in human nature. The main themes in chapter four, Book I of Kant's *Religion* are repeated in chapter one of *The Concept of Anxiety*. Specifically, Kant discusses original sin, Adam, innocence, and freedom. Kant argues that human beings freely choose to do evil and that prior conditions never necessitate an evil choice. Hence, Adam's original sin cannot necessitate the sin of any other person, otherwise there could be no freedom and hence no evil chosen. Kant's inclusion of the discussion of Adam and original sin does not entail that he accept the story of the fall as revelation, for that would not be religion within the limits of reason alone. Rather, Kant tries to show what reason can conclude regarding the fall. Just as Kant tried to show what reason could conclude regarding the fall and the origin of evil in human nature, Vigilius is here trying to use psychology in order to understand the origin of evil in human beings. Hence, he is not conflating two spheres of inquiry. Vigilius criticizes other explanations of the dogma of hereditary sin as inadequate interpretations because they are rationally inadequate. "Pious feeling and fantasy got what they demanded, a godly prelude, but thought got nothing." (CA, 25). Therefore, the first chapter does not begin with a philosophical exposition of a dogmatic concept. Rather, it begins with a philosophical rejection of any interpretation of the account of the origin of evil in human beings that is rationally inadequate.

After rejecting all such explanations, Vigilius turns to an examination of the first sin. It becomes clear in this section that for Vigilius, Adam is taken to be more than just a historical figure. More importantly, Adam is the prototype of a sinner, for Adam's first sin is similar to the first sin of every subsequent individual who sins. Hence, Vigilius uses the figure of Adam to represent the fall from innocence into sinfulness that is experienced by all subsequent individuals. This is not to say that Vigilius abandons the belief that there was an actual Adam. Rather, he ambiguously uses the figure of Adam, sometimes perhaps to refer to an actual historical first sinner, sometimes to refer to the prototype of a sinner, and sometimes to refer to the experience of first sin that is duplicated by subsequent individuals.

It is often thought that the first sin of Adam is different from every other sin, but Vigilius insists that this is only a quantitative difference. There is not a qualitative difference between the first sin of Adam and of his subsequent sins. Nor is there a qualitative difference between Adam's first sin and the sins of other people. Adam's first sin is different than every other of Adam's sins, because it is first. However, if Adam's first sin is also essentially different from every other person's first sin, then Adam is essentially different from every other person and is no longer human. Therefore, Adam's first sin is important because it is first and hence brings about a change in Adam. However, Adam's first sin is not essentially more important than any other person's first sin is to himself or herself (*CA*, 29-35).

Vigilius's main point with regard to the first sin is this. If Adam's sin necessitates sin in all other human beings, then Adam's sin is essentially different from every sin of every other person. For if this were the case, then Adam's first sin was freely chosen while everyone else sins of necessity. (Further, if everyone else sins of necessity, then they do not really sin, because sin entails freedom.) Hence, Adam's first sin is important for Adam in that through it Adam became a sinner. However, Vigilius denies that we can draw the conclusion that Adam's first sin is as important to any other individual as it is to Adam. Instead, for any individual, his or her first sin is the sin through which he or she becomes a sinner.

Given this, Vigilius recognizes that he must have an interpretation of the dogmatic view that through Adam's sin sinfulness came into the world.[10] The preceding analysis has shown that this cannot mean that Adam's sin necessitates that all humans be sinners. Vigilius interprets the teaching that "through Adam's sin, sinfulness came into the world" to mean that through Adam's first sin, sinfulness came into Adam (*CA*, 33). This interpretation saves human freedom and individual responsibility for sin. Thus, Vigilius writes:

> Through the first sin, sin came into the world. Precisely in the same way it is true of every subsequent man's first sin, that through it sin comes into the world. That it was not in the world before Adam's first sin is, in relation to sin itself, something entirely accidental and irrelevant. It is of no significance at all and cannot justify making Adam's sin greater or the first sin of every other man lesser (*CA*, 31).

Hence, there is an essential similarity between the first sin of Adam and the first sin of every other human being, for it is through the individual's first sin, and not through any external necessitating cause, that the individual becomes a sinner.

Next Vigilius turns to an analysis of the concept of innocence. Vigilius claims that innocence is a state of ignorance that precedes sin and is lost by guilt. He returns to his polemic against Hegel to insist that the relation among innocence, guilt, and redemption is not analogous to the Hegelian triad of immediacy, mediacy, and sublation. There are two main differences between the triads. First, for Hegel, immediacy is not a state; it is a nothingness that must necessarily be overcome. Vigilius insists that innocence is not a nothingness, and that it is not necessary that it be annulled. Rather, innocence is a state, albeit a state of ignorance. There is nothing in the state of innocence that necessitates that it be annulled. Further, since innocence is a state of ignorance, it does not recognize itself as innocence. Nor does innocence feel any need to be overcome. But there is a further difference between Hegel's and Vigilius's triad. On Hegel's view, immediacy and mediacy have a relationship of immanence; mediacy flows from immediacy in a successive development. This is distinguished from the state of innocence and the state of guilt. Guilt is not immanent in innocence. Rather, innocence becomes guilt by a free choice of an individual. A free choice is a leap that transcends that which preceded the choice. Therefore, guilt is not immanent in innocence in the manner of Hegelian dialectical development (*CA*, 35-8).[11]

After making it clear that innocence is a state of ignorant repose, Vigilius begins a section entitled "The Concept of the Fall." In this section, instead of accounting for the fall, his main concern is to explain what the fall is not. First, the fall is not a logical succession from the state of

innocence that preceded it. Second, the fall is not necessitated by the prohibition not to eat the fruit of the tree. If
the prohibition necessitated the fall, then the fall would
not have been the responsibility of the one who fell, nor
would it have produced guilt. Third, the fall is not necessitated by concupiscence. An analogous argument sup-
ports this claim. Concupiscence is a strong desire for that
which is prohibited. However, it is not necessary for the
individual to act upon this desire. If concupiscence
necessitated the fall, then the fall would not have been
the responsibility of the one who fell, nor would it have
produced guilt. Even if the prohibition intensifies concupiscence, neither the prohibition nor the concupiscence
necessitate the fall (*CA*, 38-41).

Vigilius is again at pains to maintain the distinction
between psychology and dogmatics. The most psychology can do is transcendentally explain the fall by explaining the state of the individual that is the condition for the
possibility of the fall. This state does not necessitate the
fall. The fall is a choice that is not necessitated by any
pre-existing condition.[12]

Next, Vigilius turns to describe the psychological state
of the individual that preceded the fall and is the condition for the possibility of the fall. That condition is anxiety. This section of chapter one is, for the most part, one
of the clearest sections of the book, as well as one of the
most influential for 20th century existentialist thinkers.

The view of the self that Vigilius sets forth in this
section is a necessary preliminary to a complete understanding of the concept of anxiety. In the third section of
this chapter, Vigilius analyzed the concept of innocence
and showed that innocence is a state of ignorant repose.
Here, Vigilius holds to and uses that analysis but looks at
the structure of the human being who is in repose. Vigilius
states that a human being "is a synthesis of the psychical
and the physical" (*CA*, 43). These two poles include not

only body and mind, but also future and past, possibility and necessity, finitude and infinitude. These two poles are united by a third, namely spirit. Spirit is the power of the will to self-consciously relate the two poles of the synthesis to one another and hence to the self. The innocent person has not done anything to relate the psychical and physical to one another. For example, the innocent person has not imagined future possibilities and chosen from among them. The part of the self that chooses in such cases is the spirit. Since the innocent person has not chosen in such a fashion, Vigilius says the spirit in such a person is dreaming. This is Vigilius's manner of saying that the power of choosing is a potential power that has not yet been actualized for the innocent person. If he were to deny that the innocent person has a spirit, and thus, no ability to choose at all, then he could not account for the possibility of the innocent person's free transition out of innocence into guilt. Hence, the person in innocence is said to be one in whom spirit is dreaming.

The future does not yet exist for the person in innocence. It is a nothing. The relation of the innocent person to the nothingness of future possibilities is anxiety. Anxiety must be distinguished from fear. First, the person does not fear future possibilities, for there is nothing to fear. Fear is a relationship to a definite something. Anxiety is the relation between the person and future possibilities, which are a nothingness. Second, fear consists solely in repulsion. However, anxiety involves two elements: repulsion and attraction.

Anxiety, which is this relation between the person and nothingness, is an ambiguous relation. It is both an attraction and a repulsion. Hence, Vigilius writes "Anxiety is *a sympathetic antipathy* and *an antipathetic sympathy*" (*CA*, 42). This is shown by several examples. The person who looks over a cliff experiences anxiety, for such a person is repelled by the thought of falling off the cliff, and yet there is almost an urge to jump (*CA*, 61). So too, when the prohibition is given to Adam, Adam is both attracted to that which is prohibited and at the same time repelled by it (*CA*, 44). Hence, anxiety is central to freedom of choice, for the person who looks over the edge of the cliff is neither necessitated to jump nor to stand still, though both are possible. Thus, Vigilius writes "anxiety is freedom's actuality as the possibility of possibility" (*CA*, 44), meaning anxiety makes possibility possible and hence makes freedom actual. For where there is no possibility, there is no freedom.[13]

Anxiety is central to understanding the sin of Adam, for the psychological state is the condition for the possibility of sin. Adam reacts to the prohibition with anxiety. He is both attracted to the forbidden fruit and repelled from it. His anxiety did not necessitate his sin; rather, through it he had the experience of "being able." This experience of being able to disobey does not necessitate that he disobey. Hence, anxiety does not necessitate sin. Nor is anxiety the sin. No matter how much Adam is attracted to the forbidden fruit, he is still related to the eating of it as a future possibility in anxiety. He is still, at least in a small way, repelled from disobeying (*CA*, 44). Because of this ambiguity in anxiety, the anxiety does not cause the choice. Rather, anxiety is the condition for the possibility of the choice.

To be sure, the term anxiety is sometimes used by Vigilius to refer to an affective state. The person who looks over the edge of the cliff feels anxious; there is both the dizzying feeling that one might fall with its accompanying repulsion and a quietly felt urge to lean out farther, to leap. Yet, Vigilius's analysis of anxiety goes beyond a description of these affective states. In describing the human being as a synthesis of the psychical and the physical united by spirit, he provides an analysis of the structure of human being. Given this structural analysis of human being, the psychical aspect can imagine future possibilities based on one's present and past (the physical aspect). The structural relation between one's present and imagined future possibilities is a relation of anxiety. This is an ontological claim, a claim that the way a human being is related to the future is through the ambiguity of simultaneous attraction and repulsion. In this sense, anxiety is not a description of how one feels, but of a person's relation to the future. As we will see, this relation remains, even when the affect is not felt. When the term "anxiety" is used in this ontological sense, it means that one's relation to the future is one of freedom, since no one future possibility is a necessity. Therefore, the term "anxiety" refers to an ontological structure of human being, specifically one's free relation to the future.

Finally, when Vigilius uses the term "anxiety" in this sense, as one's free relation to the future when one is both attracted to and repulsed from the nothingness of future possibilities, he is not describing a sickness. Too often Kierkegaard commentators have missed the significance of this point.[14] The innocent individual is also in a state of anxiety. If anxiety were a sickness in the self, or even a symptom of a disease in the self, then that would mean either that Adam is not innocent prior to the fall or that the fall is a logical development of a prior state. But Vigilius has claimed that neither of these is the case. Therefore, it must be that anxiety is neither a symptom of a diseased self nor a sickness in the self.[15] Rather, anxiety, which is one's ambiguous relation to future possibilities, is the normal state of the innocent person. Anxiety comes to be related with sickness not because it itself is a sickness, but because it is the condition for the possibility of the first sin, both in Adam and in every other individual. As we will see, Kierkegaard claims that sin, not anxiety, is a sickness of the self.

In the sixth and final section of the first chapter of *The Concept of Anxiety*, Vigilius summarizes the first chapter. Anxiety explains the concept of hereditary sin only insofar as it is the state of the individual prior to the first sin. Psychology is unable to provide a causal explanation of the fall, since sin is a free act incapable of a complete causal explanation. Hence, the first chapter was not an attempt to give a causal explanation of sin; rather, it sought through a transcendental explanation to understand the origin of sin in human beings by psychologically examining anxiety, which is the state that precedes but does not necessitate the first sin and hence is the condition for the possibility of sin.

3. Anxiety as Explaining Hereditary Sin

The Western Christian tradition has virtually always been forced to explain the problem of original sin.[16] After St. Augustine, the problem has usually been framed by the following question: "How can a person both inherit sin and be responsible for it?" Some Kierkegaard commentators assumed that Kierkegaard accepts this as a paradox of faith (Thulstrup 1980, 122-56). However, in chapter two of *The Concept of Anxiety* Vigilius treats the problem of hereditary sin as a dilemma to be solved. He does not accept it as a paradox of faith.

Earlier we saw that Vigilius holds the following points. Adam is essentially similar to every person. Sin entered into Adam through Adam's own sin. Particular sins are inexplicable. Adam is the prototype of a sinner, not the cause of sin in any other person. Sin enters in every other person through that person's own sin. Given these conclusions, the traditional paradox of original sin has been resolved. Individuals are not guilty for a sin they did not commit, e.g., Adam's original sin. Instead, every individual who has sinned is guilty only of his or her own sins.

The issue might become clearer if we contrast it with a typical misunderstanding of Kierkegaard's view on guilt and original sin. Many commentators have made sense of Kierkegaard's discussion of these topics by referring to Søren's father, Michael Pederson Kierkegaard. The story is told that the father, while eleven years old, was tending his flocks on the Jutland heath. He was alone, wet, cold and hungry. He raised his eyes to the gray heavens and cursed God for making an innocent child suffer. Afterward, apparently he felt tremendously guilty for his act and thought that he and all his offspring would be damned for this sin (Thompson 1973, 23). Moreover, the father must have also felt tremendous guilt regarding Søren's mother.

Michael Pederson Kierkegaard married Kirstine Royen, his social equal, in 1794. Two years later she died without having had any children. Before the year was over and while he should have still been mourning the death of his wife, his maid (Søren's mother to be) became pregnant. Based on the birth date of the child, she must have conceived in December of 1796. The father probably found out that his maid was pregnant in January or February of 1797. In February of that year, he retired from business and took up pietistic theology. We can only imagine the guilt and confusion that he must have experienced, for he married his maid just two months later, in April. Five months after the marriage, a daughter was born. During this time, he immersed himself in reading pietistic theology. He saw himself and his offspring as guilty for his sins. (Søren was the youngest of seven children born of this second marriage.)

Søren Kierkegaard may have been strongly influenced by his father, but he apparently did not hold the same view as him on hereditary sin. The father apparently held that sin was passed on from generation to generation, that sin is literally hereditary. Vigilius, in chapter one, re-

jects that view. If subsequent individuals are not guilty of
Adam's sins, then neither are Michael Pederson
Kierkegaard's children guilty of his sins. Hence if, as some
commentators have urged,[17] Kierkegaard's writing is some-
how a dialogue with his parents or his father, then *The
Concept of Anxiety* is a rejection of his father's view that
children are guilty for the sins of their fathers. Of course,
it does not follow from this that Søren Kierkegaard is
declaring himself innocent. To be sure, he recognized
himself as guilty, and as a sinner. However, if he is to
embrace the view that he has Vigilius set forth in *The
Concept of Anxiety*, then he is guilty only for his own
sins—not the sin of Adam, and not the sins of his father.

Still, it is not completely satisfactory to view chapter
one of *The Concept of Anxiety* simply as a rejection of his
father's views on the "hereditariness" of original sin. Rather,
the view that Vigilius sets forth is a rejection of an entire
way of interpreting hereditary sin.

Given this, we can see that Vigilius's view of original
sin is more radical than has often been recognized. Vigilius
has reframed the entire issue of original sin. According to
Vigilius, the individual does not participate in original sin
through relation to Adam. Most prior explanations of original sin sought to explain the sins of subsequent individuals
through their relation to Adam. Vigilius holds that the individual participates in original sin through a relation to sin.
Having sinned, one has participated in original sin through
an experience essentially similar to Adam's first sin.

The problem Vigilius now faces is explaining in what
sense original sin is hereditary. For in chapter one, Vigilius
has dissolved the traditional dilemma that arises with the
Western Christian notion of original sin, namely, blaming
people for a sin they did not commit. However, he has
created a new problem. His new problem is primarily a
theological issue, for traditional theology claims that
Adam's sin is significant not only for Adam, but also for

all humans. Still, a philosophical issue is involved. Does each individual exist in complete isolation from every other individual, or do individuals affect one another? If so, to what extent? In chapter two, Vigilius takes up the task of showing the sense in which Adam's sin quantitatively changes the situation that all subsequent individuals face, without necessitating that we become sinners. In doing so, he guards against the charge of radical individualism without sacrificing either freedom of choice or personal responsibility for one's acts.

Adam's sin had several effects. Sin entered into the world by his becoming a sinner. This does not obliterate anxiety, for the person in sin still has an ambiguous relation to the future possibility of either sinning again or being redeemed. Hence, anxiety keeps its basic structure of both attraction to and repulsion from future possibilities, but there is a change in anxiety since there is an important change in future possibilities.

Vigilius refuses to claim that one of the effects of Adam's first sin is the sinfulness of the rest of the human race. Instead, the two main effects of Adam's sin are to change the world and to change the intensity of the desire that subsequent innocent individuals experience. Vigilius terms these objective and subjective anxiety.

The section on objective anxiety is initially very perplexing. Vincent McCarthy claims it is the weakest section in the book; he assumes that it is taken up only so there will be some contrast for the following section on subjective anxiety (1978, 41). However, McCarthy does not make clear that in this section Vigilius is trying to make sense of the "hereditariness" of sin. In chapter one, the view that sin is strictly hereditary, that is, that it causes a flaw in the being of subsequent individuals, is rejected. In this section, Vigilius discusses the way sin and anxiety enter into the social context and the historical nexus and hence the way sin and anxiety become objectified.[18]

Haufniensis recognizes that, after Adam, individuals are not born into an environment in which sin is absent. Rather, innocent individuals are born into a world with parents who are themselves sinners, a world with distorted social structures, and in specific historical situations that are more or less complicated by wrongdoing. In this sense, anxiety has become objectified. Here, Vigilius may be shifting the meaning of "anxiety," for it is not so much anxiety that becomes objectified, but sinfulness. Thus, when Vigilius writes about objective anxiety, he has shifted his meaning so that he is referring to sinful social structures that become objectified as they take root and people participate in them. In different cultures, anxiety becomes objectified in different ways,[19] which is to say that in different societies, sinfulness has different expressions.

With each successive generation, the quantity of sinfulness and anxiety in the world increases. These increases in quantity affect each new innocent individual, though they do not qualitatively change the innocent individual (*CA*, 57). This means that for each individual, though the person is born into a home with parents who are themselves sinners and into a distorted social context, it is not the parents or the social context alone that causes this person to sin. If the person becomes a sinner, it is through a free act. The fact that there is an increased quantity of sin and anxiety in the world, which is begun by Adam and is continued by every sinner's sin, is not alone what caused the person to sin. The qualitative change in the person, the move from innocence to guilt, is always a free act of the individual. The individual who is guilty is always, at least in part, responsible for his or her sinfulness.

There are always two elements involved when an innocent person becomes guilty. On the one hand, there is the fall by the person into sin. On the other hand, there is the context in which the fall into sin occurs. "Objective anxiety" is Vigilius's term for the increase in sinfulness in the world that is one part of the fall into guilt for all individuals subsequent to Adam.

The section on subjective anxiety continues the attempt to show the significance of Adam's first sin and to explain some further sense in which sin accumulates in the world without making Adam responsible for the sin of any subsequent individual. Vigilius explains that while the object of anxiety for Adam was the nothingness of the future, for subsequent individuals this future nothingness has a more specific form, or as he phrases it, is more of a "something" (*CA*, 61). Haufniensis terms this "subjective anxiety" and claims it signifies two things (*CA*, 62).

The first thing that the change in the object of anxiety signifies is the consequence of the relationship of generation. Adam's sin (treating Adam here as a historical figure) did not take place in a developed social structure, or at least not in one that had been distorted by human sinfulness. Yet the movement from innocence to guilt that is made by subsequent individuals is made in a distorted social structure. Hence, for subsequent individuals, anxiety is in a certain sense more intensified than it was for Adam. For example, suppose a person is born into a family and a society with a distorted social structure. At some point the person may move from innocence to guilt, perhaps by taking on a distorted role in that social structure. The experience of moving from innocence to guilt will be similar to Adam's in that it was a free act. No science can observe in others what the guilty individual himself or herself knows, i.e., personal responsibility. Like Adam's first sin, the movement of the individual from innocence to guilt was made by an inexplicable leap. However, this person's experience is different from Adam's because of the consequence of the relation to the social setting in which the person was placed. The anxiety of this person is different from the anxiety of Adam in that the object of anxiety, which is the future possibility of actively taking part in this distorted social structure, is more developed than the object of anxiety for Adam.

To explain this point, Vigilius uses the figure of Eve, since she was derived from Adam.[20] Unfortunately, his discussion of the role of women is annoyingly sexist, even by 19th century standards. However, his discussion of the role of women is not the main point; instead it is used as an example to explain an important difference between Adam's anxiety and the anxiety of subsequent individuals. The difference is that for subsequent individuals, anxiety's object, while still a future possibility, is more concrete, since it is the possibility of actively taking part in a distorted social structure that is already in place. The conclusion of this section is best summed up when Vigilius writes: "Christianity has never assented to giving each particular individual the privilege of starting from the beginning in an external sense. Each individual begins in an historical nexus" (*CA*, 73). Since every subsequent individual begins in a specific historical nexus that is already more or less distorted, the future possibility of actively taking part in that social structure is a more concrete possibility than the possibility that Adam faced. This, then, is an important difference between the first sin of Adam and every other sin. Still, this is a quantitative difference in anxiety, not a qualitative difference.[21]

The second thing that the change in the object of anxiety signifies is the consequence of the historical relationship. The anxiety of an innocent person may have various objects, depending on the historical setting in which the innocent person has been placed. To explain his point, Vigilius discusses sensuality.

There is nothing intrinsically evil about sensuality; there is nothing wrong with being a bodily creature. However, one of the consequences of sin is that it makes sensuousness sinful. (Thus, although Vigilius rejects any austere Augustinianism which makes being bodily intrinsically bad, he does not replace it with an optimistic Pelagianism.) Sinfulness makes sensuality sinfulness. Therefore, there is an important difference between the first sin of Adam and the first sin of every subsequent individual regarding their respective views of sensuality. In the garden and while in innocence, Adam had no insight that the body was shameful. It was sin which made sensuousness to be sinfulness. However, the situation is different for people in different historical settings. Subsequent individuals have "an historical environment in which it may become apparent that sensuousness can signify sinfulness. For the [innocent] individual himself, sensuousness does not signify this, but this knowledge gives anxiety a 'more'" (*CA*, 73). This means that there can be an important difference between the anxiety of Adam and the anxiety of subsequent innocent individuals regarding their knowledge of the possibility of making sensuousness sinfulness. Further, this intensification in anxiety can vary in different societies. For example, the knowledge that an innocent person in a Christian society has of the possibility of making sensuousness to be sinfulness might vary from the same knowledge that an innocent person would have in a different society (*CA*, 74). Thus, the historical environment in which one is placed can make a difference in affecting the intensity of the anxiety. Still, this is always a quantitative difference. It is never enough to make an innocent person guilty without some act of personal responsibility on the part of the person who becomes guilty.

In summing up this chapter, Vigilius claims that there are three main ways of misunderstanding the role that the individual plays in becoming guilty (*CA*, 75-6). The first possible mistake is to view the child as a "perfect little angel" who is plunged into a corrupt society. The child is so strongly influenced by this distorted environment that, of necessity, the child is made bad. But this view fails to recognize what the guilty individual alone knows: per-

sonal responsibility played a role in choosing to participate actively in this distorted social setting. Hence, Kierkegaard implicitly rejects Rousseau's view on the nature of
human beings and the effect of the environment upon
them.

The second possible mistake is to view the child as
thoroughly wicked. But this view fails to recognize the
possibility of an innocence that preceded wickedness and
hence it must place responsibility on something other than
the guilty individual. Therefore, Kierkegaard rejects an
austere Augustinianism or Hobbesian view on the innate
wickedness of persons.

The third possible mistake is to view the child as neither good nor bad though capable of each, depending
solely on how the child is environmentally conditioned.
Again, this view ignores the possibility of personal responsibility. In this way, Kierkegaard implicitly rejects B.F.
Skinner's view on the role of the environment in conditioning the individual. Vigilius's view — that the child is
born in innocence but into a sinful society and that, in
anxiety, the individual freely chooses evil — avoids the
mistakes of each of these views by including a middle
term: anxiety.

Chapter two is therefore important at several levels.
Theologically, Vigilius shows the sense in which Adam's
first sin is significant. Adam's sin brings sin into the world
and hence changes the object of anxiety for subsequent
individuals. This intensification of anxiety in subsequent
individuals is "the presence of hereditary sin in the single
individual" (CA, 52). This does not mean that the anxiety
is itself sin. Vigilius constantly reminds us that the presence of this intensified anxiety does not necessitate sin.
Thus, hereditary sin is not a flaw in one's being caused
by Adam's sin, as most earlier interpretations have understood it. Rather, hereditary sin consists in the double fact
that sin and anxiety get objectified in distorted social struc-

tures and that the innocent individual has a quantitatively increased relation in anxiety to the future possibility of actively participating in that distorted society in a distorted way. In this way, Vigilius has solved the traditional dilemma of original sin. Individuals are guilty only for their own guilty acts. However, there is still a sense in which the dogma of hereditary sin is true, for there is the double fact that sin and anxiety quantitatively accumulate in the world, and that such an objectification of anxiety in the world quantitatively increases anxiety in subsequent individuals.

At a philosophical and psychological level, chapter two is a defense against the charge of radical individualism. Haufniensis makes it clear that individuals are always placed in particular environments with unique social settings in a specific historical nexus. He wholeheartedly admits that the environment conditions the individual, for it intensifies anxiety by giving its object a more concrete form, i.e., the possibility of accepting or rejecting the specific distorted social context. This is what Vigilius means when he writes that the nothing of anxiety is made into a something (*CA*, 61). Still, the environment never wholly determines the individual. This is what Vigilius means when he says that the something is still a nothing (*CA*, 61). The individual has an ambiguous relationship to future possibilities, a relationship of both attraction and repulsion. Even if the individual has a fairly concrete image of these future possibilities, e.g., of either accepting or rejecting the possibility of actively taking part in a distorted social structure, the individual is not necessitated to do either. However, if the individual does make the leap into guiltiness, the condition for the possibility of that leap was anxiety.

4. Anxiety and the Absence of the Consciousness of Sin

In chapter two, Vigilius stated that in different historical settings, anxiety takes different forms (*CA*, 73-6). Now, in chapter three, Haufniensis describes three forms of anxiety that typify different settings. The basic structure of anxiety remains the same in each: anxiety is both the attraction to and the repulsion from still undetermined future possibilities. In the case of Adam, his anxiety had to do with the prohibition not to eat the fruit from the tree. Now the scene is changed. The people described in this chapter are not in innocence. However, in none of the settings that Vigilius describes in this chapter is there a consciousness of sin. Thus, chapter three is a description of three forms of anxiety that are typified in different distorted societies where there is not a consciousness of sin.

Implicit in this chapter is the view that there are two main ways to sin. The first way is not to be conscious that one is sinning. This not being conscious that one is sinning is itself a sin. The second way to sin is to do so consciously. In this chapter, Vigilius limits himself to the former kind of sinning. He discusses the latter in chapter four.

There is a long preamble in this chapter that precedes the description of these three forms of anxiety. This introductory section is primarily a review of earlier material and a further explanation of Vigilius's understanding of the self. Haufniensis has already explained that the self is a synthesis of the body and the soul that is sustained by spirit (*CA*, 43). Vigilius now further explains the role of both time and eternity in the self. In order to understand this section, it is necessary to realize that Vigilius's view of the self is both ontological and normative. In an ontological sense, the self *is* a synthesis of two poles that is willfully sustained through spirit. However, in a normative sense, the self has itself as a task; it has an obligation to achieve the synthesis for itself. This task is something that lies before it and hence is the object of anxiety. This means that a spirit that sustains the synthesis in the self is both what the self is and what it ought to be. The self is a synthesis of the temporal and eternal in the self, and yet it is only through taking up the task of becoming a self that the future comes to be meaningful.

Because of this double meaning in the self, that the self both is and yet ought to be achieved, Vigilius can refer to spiritlessness without contradiction. Spiritlessness is the failure to take up becoming oneself as a task. Human spiritlessness is different from animal spiritlessness in that non-human animals do not have the potential to form themselves willfully, as humans do. Thus, when Vigilius refers to spiritlessness, he uses the term primarily in a normative, not an ontological sense.

The first form of anxiety described in chapter three is the anxiety of spiritlessness. Spiritlessness is the human failure to recognize that one's task is to achieve selfhood, that is, to form oneself. As such, spiritlessness is a failure to recognize the future. Therefore, since anxiety is an ambiguous relationship to the future, there is no felt affect of anxiety experienced in the anxiety of spiritlessness. However, this is only how it appears from the viewpoint of spiritlessness. From the viewpoint of spirit, where one recognizes the failure in spiritlessness, one can also recognize that there is an ignored relationship to the future in spiritlessness. Therefore, "viewed from the standpoint of spirit, anxiety is also present in spiritlessness, but it is hidden and disguised" (CA, 96). The person in spiritlessness who ignores the task of becoming a self may have no feeling of anxiety; still, since the person is a human being, there is an anxious relationship to the future. This ignored relationship to the future is the anxiety of spiritlessness. Vigilius mentions Christian paganism as an example of people who typify the anxiety of spiritlessness. "Christian paganism" is Vigilius's term for people who live in a Christian society but have become dulled to Christianity and fail to recognize their task to form their lives and become selves.

Next, Vigilius describes the form of anxiety defined dialectically as fate. Vigilius claims that in ancient Greek and Oriental cultures, the object of anxiety is a supposed fate (CA, 97). In order to explain himself, Haufniensis uses the example of the genius. The theme of the genius was not uncommon in 19th century literature. Vigilius uses this theme, particularly with Napoleon in mind, to explain his description of the anxiety of fate (CA, 99). The genius is dependent upon a supposed fate to give a signal. For example, in the case of a military genius, the signal concerns when to begin the battle (CA, 99). While waiting for the sign from fate, the genius has an ambiguous relationship to the future, for it is both loved and feared. Thus, the genius who is dependent on fate is anxious. This sort of anxiety, according to Vigilius, typifies Oriental and Greek cultures, which are dependent on fate.

The third form of anxiety described in this chapter is typified, according to Vigilius, in Judaism. He refers to this form of anxiety as that which is defined dialectically as guilt. Here the individual sees before oneself the future possibility of guilt. "As freedom with all its passion wishfully stares at itself and would keep guilt at a distance so that not a single particle of it might be found in freedom, it cannot refrain from staring at guilt, and this staring is the ambiguous staring of anxiety, just as renunciation within the possibility is itself a coveting" (CA, 109). This sort of anxiety is quantitatively different from the anxiety of Adam, for the future possibility in such cases is not just an unknown nothing, but is more concrete. "Guilt is a more concrete conception, which becomes more and more possible in the relation of possibility to freedom"

(*CA*, 109). Thus, the anxiety of guilt is the simultaneous attraction to and repulsion from the possibility of guilt.

In conclusion, chapter three is more descriptive than either of the preceding chapters. The anxiety described is the anxiety that typifies particular cultural circumstances. Each of the settings is the consequence of sin. The first is a society in which there is a failure to recognize that humans have a task to become selves. The anxiety that typifies this setting is not recognized as anxiety by those in it, for there is no conscious relation to the future. Still, there is an ignored relation to the future. This ignored relation to the future is the anxiety of spiritlessness. The second is a society in which the future is viewed as fated. The anxiety that typifies such a society is a simultaneous attraction to and repulsion from fate, both to love and to fear it. The third is a society in which guilt reigns. Here, the individual is both attracted to and repulsed from guilt. The individuals in each of these settings have no clear recognition of sin. In this way, chapter three is a description of three forms of anxiety which are the consequence of sin, but the sin in question is precisely that there is no consciousness of sin.

5. *The Anxiety of Sin*

In the preceding section, there was a distinction drawn between two kinds of sinning: not being conscious that one is sinning, and consciously sinning. Vigilius discussed the former in chapter three. In chapter four, he describes the latter.

In both chapters, Vigilius is describing particular forms of anxiety. This is crucially important, and it is a point on which not all Kierkegaard commentators have been clear.[22] Haufniensis is here describing the anxiety of one who is in sin. In order to do this, he must also briefly describe the sinful state of such a person, but he does so only because there is a conceptual connection between sin and the anxiety of sin: a description of the anxiety of sin is parasitic upon some description of sin. The key point is that this is a chapter describing a particular form of anxiety, namely that which is the consequence of sin in the single individual.

Chapter four begins with an explanation of why anxiety continues even after sin. One might assume that anxiety would disappear after sin since anxiety is freedom's disclosure to itself as possibility. Sin is an actuality, so why doesn't this actuality annul the possibility of anxiety? There are several reasons (*CA*, 111-12). First, one still has an ambiguous relation to the future. Also, the actuality of sin is an unwarranted actuality, and hence it does not overcome the possibility of anxiety. Therefore, even after sin there is anxiety. Anxiety retains its same basic structure: it is still the simultaneous attraction to and repulsion from future possibilities. However, with sin comes a change in the person and a change in one's future possibilities. Therefore, the chapter is a description of the anxiety that is the consequence of sin.

Such an anxiety can have one of two objects as a future possibility: good or evil. Vigilius describes three forms of the anxiety of evil. The first form is to be both attracted to and repulsed from continuing in sin (*CA*, 113). The second is both to love and fear the possibility of sinking more deeply into sin, for no matter how deeply one has sunk, it is always possible to sink further (*CA*, 113-5). The third form of the anxiety of evil is both to love and fear the sorrow and grief associated with repentance (*CA*, 115-7).

The second possible object of an anxiety that is the consequence of sin is the good. In the section on the anxiety of the good, Vigilius deviates from psychological description and develops the themes of the demonic, inwardness, the moment, and earnestness. His treatment of them is somewhat independent of his description of the anxiety about the good. Therefore, my discussion of this section will focus on the psychological description of anxiety about the good.

The key to understanding this form of anxiety is to recall the chapter in which it is included. The chapter title, "Anxiety of Sin," tells us that this is a form of anxiety found in those who have sinned. This is not to say that the anxiety about the good is itself the sin. Rather, the person who experiences this form of anxiety is in sin and is faced with the future possibility of redemption. Here, Vigilius describes how the person in sin is repulsed from the possibility of redemption. And yet, no matter how strong this repulsion is, there is still a longing for the possibility of redemption. This repulsion from the good and denial of the possibility of redemption is what Vigilius calls the demonic. The demonic is not primarily an attraction to evil, but a repulsion from good (*CA*, 119). Vigilius's term for closing oneself off from the good is *indesluttede*. Thomte translates it as "inclosing reserve" while Lowrie translates it "shutupness." Both translations are clumsy. The concept involved is that of closing oneself off or turning inward and away from external help. For example, if someone were drowning and they had a floating life preserver thrown to them, and they swam away from it, refusing help, they would be turning away from assistance. In the case of *indesluttede*, the same turning away occurs psychologically. The individual turns in on oneself and away from external aid. Even in this extreme form of sin, when an individual defiantly refuses the possibility of redemption, there is anxiety, for while the individual clearly is repulsed by the possibility of redemption, the individual "always retains a relation [with the good], and even when this has apparently disappeared altogether, it is nevertheless there, and anxiety at once manifests itself in the moment of contact [with the good]" (*CA*, 123).

Here again it is evident that Vigilius is using the term "anxiety" to refer to an ontological structure of human being and not just to a felt affect. Intermittent feelings of anxiety are grounded in the structure of anxiety that is one's ambiguous relationship with the future. The demonic person who is closed off and shut up and refuses the possibility of redemption does not feel anxious until there is some explicit contact with the good. The gospels show this in that the demonic was usually mute until there was contact with Christ. When a demonic person came into contact with Christ, anxiety showed itself. Hence, though the demonic person may become so closed up that there is no feeling of anxiety, there is yet an ambiguous relation to the future and to the good. This structural relation to the future, a relation of ambiguity, is anxiety, and it shows itself intermittently in the feeling of anxiety (*CA*, 123).

Anxiety about the good, therefore, like the other forms of anxiety discussed in the third and fourth chapters of *The Concept of Anxiety*, is a particular form of anxiety experienced by people who are in a particular form of sin. The person is conscious of herself or himself as a person in sin. The object of anxiety is the good, in particular, the possibility of redemption, salvation or the restoration of freedom (*CA*, 119). The individual's relation to this future possibility is ambiguous, for the individual is both attracted to it and repulsed from it. This is true no matter how far the individual has turned away from the good and denied the possibility of redemption. Even in the extreme case, where the person has closed herself or himself off from the good, the person still, as it were, notices the good out of the corner of one's eye. Despite the fact that the person immediately turns away from the good, the sensitive psychologist recognizes that there is still a faint attraction to the good. Hence, while anxiety about the good is primarily characterized by a repulsion from the good, the ambiguous character common to all forms of anxiety is still present, since the person is still slightly attracted to the good.

6. Anxiety as Saving Through Faith

The final chapter in *The Concept of Anxiety* is a brief analysis of a beneficial use of anxiety. In this chapter, Vigilius claims that when anxiety is understood and used properly, it can be educative for human life and an aid in salvation.

Anxiety entails imagining future possibilities and being both attracted to and repulsed from them.[23] These possibilities are not just finite somethings, but include the whole array of future possibilities that do not yet exist. If one has a proper understanding of anxiety, it can be educative in at least three ways. First, it can help one better understand the relationship between possibility and actuality. To be educated by anxiety is to be educated by possibility. Possibility is usually seen to be of little significance when compared with actuality. However, for one who is educated by anxiety, it becomes evident that in a certain sense, possibility is more significant than actuality. Actuality, which is the sum of what is past and is now present, is no longer in the control of the individual. While what is actual conditions what is possible, it is not the only conditioning factor. Through an understanding of the concept of anxiety, one comes to see that the individual, through choice, is able to choose from among future possibilities that do not yet exist and make them actual. In this way, possibility is more significant to the individual than is actuality (*CA*, 156). For example, in choosing between two courses of life — whether to attend this school or that, whether to accept this offer of marriage or not — future possibilities are imagined, and one can sense that either set of possibilities will make an enormous difference in shaping the tapestry of one's life.

At this moment in one's life, these future possibilities, and how one chooses among them, are of greater significance than the mundane facticity of the here and now.

The second way that anxiety can be educative is that through possibility, one is able to imagine an infinity of life forms. The type of anxiety that Vigilius has been describing throughout the book has to do with imagining future possibilities. Thus, the one who is able to imagine future possibilities is freed from the error of Carpocratianism. The Carpocratians were a heretical second century Gnostic sect who held that in order to attain perfection, a person must first participate in the worst human experiences.[24] This group heretically held that experiencing all the vices was necessary for salvation. Vigilius rejects this sort of approach. There is no need to experience all of the vices as long as one is educated by possibility, for one can gain an adequate experience of them through one's imagination. This is a point often associated with Kierkegaard, that through the power of imagination one can imagine various life forms and spheres of existence and play them out in possibility to gain a better understanding of them. Vigilius writes "Take the pupil of possibility, place him in the middle of the Jutland heath, where no event takes place or where the greatest event is a grouse flying up noisily, and he will experience everything more perfectly, more accurately, more thoroughly than the man who received the applause on the stage of world-history if that man was not educated by possibility" (*CA*, 159). Thus, one can be educated by anxiety in the sense that anxiety is a necessary ingredient in imagining various possible life forms.

The third way that anxiety can be educative is through insight into one's guilt. Through an understanding of anxiety, one can come to see that if one is guilty, then one is infinitely guilty. Infinitude does not here refer to a very large quantity; rather, it signifies a qualitative change. Infinitude is usually a spatial metaphor, but it is used here as a temporal metaphor. Vigilius is not denying that some acts are more grave than others. Rather, he is affirming that once one has become guilty, one can never go back in history to become innocent again. The leap into guilt is one for which the individual is responsible and one which brings about a qualitative change in the individual, from innocence to guilt. One who does not have an adequate understanding of anxiety may view guilt in a strictly finite sense. For example, a person may see guilt only as a relation to something external, for example, as to "judgements of the police court and the supreme court" (*CA*, 161). But the person who understands anxiety and the leap into guilt understands that "if a man is guilty, he is infinitely guilty" (*CA*, 161). This does not mean that the person who is guilty is incapable of anything but corrupt acts; instead it means that the guilty person cannot make himself or herself innocent again. Once a choice is acted upon, there is no going back. That's the rub of anxiety, because once the leap is made, it becomes a part of one's history. It cannot be undone.

The book ends with the insight that through anxiety one comes to understand oneself as infinitely guilty. However, Vigilius does not take this to be depressing. Rather, having been educated by possibility of one's infinite guilt, one can better understand the need for atonement (*CA*, 162). Thus, while the book is a psychological deliberation on the concept of anxiety, it is done as an aid to dogmatics. Its aim is to improve one's understanding of the dogmatic issue of hereditary sin, and ultimately to deepen one's understanding of the need for atonement.

7. *The Incompleteness of* The Concept of Anxiety

The Concept of Anxiety is often said to be Kierkegaard's most difficult work. This is understandable. First, it is a seminal, ground breaking work. There is no earlier work that philosophically examines the concept of anxiety in order to gain insight into the dogmatic issue of hereditary sin. Second, some of the examples used in the book are difficult to understand. Too often the example is more difficult to understand than the point the example is supposed to explain. Part of the explanation of this is that contemporary readers do not have the same background as did Kierkegaard. However, part of this is surely that Kierkegaard only infrequently has Vigilius make explicit how a particular example is supposed to illuminate a particular point. Finally, this work is difficult because it spans several disciplines. It is neither solely a philosophical treatise nor is it solely a theological one. While the book uses a "psychological" method, the content overlaps with the domains of theology and to a lesser extent with philosophical ethics. The first point, that the work is seminal, partly explains its difficulty. The second point, the difficulty in understanding its use of examples, further explains its complexity and places some of the blame on Kierkegaard. However, the final point, the complexity of topics covered, itself requires a more complete explanation.

In the second section of this chapter, I argued that though there appears to be a contradiction between the introduction and chapters one and two of *The Concept of Anxiety*, there is no real contradiction. In the introduction, Vigilius claims both that one should not conflate spheres of study and that *The Concept of Anxiety* is a work in psychology but not dogmatics. In chapters one and two there is a good deal of discussion of the dogmatic issue of hereditary sin. The reason there is no contradiction here is that the admonition was against using the method of one study to draw a conclusion in another. For example, one should not use the method of psychology to draw a conclusion about dogmatics. Vigilius does not, and I think correctly, see himself as doing this. Rather, he sees himself as using the method of psychology, that is, the method of observation and explanation, to clarify our understanding of the human state that precedes sin. He recognizes that this information will be of great interest to Christians concerned with the dogmatic issues of sin and hereditary sin. However, his goal in this book is to draw psychological, not theological, conclusions.

The reason that this is so complicated is that throughout the book, Vigilius is describing the state of anxiety in people who are either in sin or are anxious about the possibility of sin. Since Vigilius takes sin to be a dogmatic category, (*CA*, 14-20) he omits any explanation or definition of the concept of sin. This can leave the reader confused. Vigilius has refused to explain or define the dogmatic concept of sin, for he is not writing a dogmatic work, but the reader of *The Concept of Anxiety* is left with a well developed understanding of the concept of anxiety, but one that is dependent on a thoroughly unexplained concept of sin. Therefore, as it stands, *The Concept of Anxiety* is a work which needs a complementary analysis of the concept of sin.

The more fully developed analysis of the concept of sin is to be found in the second part of *The Sickness Unto Death*. Sin is there understood to be despair before God. I shall turn now to an analysis of the concepts of despair and sin, especially as they are explained in *The Sickness Unto Death*.

A Preparatory Examination of Several Topics Related to *The Sickness Unto Death*

1. *The Danish Term* Fortvivlelse

The Danish term *fortvivlelse* has virtually always been translated into English as despair. Still, there are etymological differences between the English "despair" and the Danish "*fortvivlelse*" and these are worth exploring in order to make as clear as possible Kierkegaard's understanding of the term.[1]

The English word "despair" has a French and Latin origin; it means literally "without hope."[2] On the other hand, the Danish term *fortvivlelse* has a German origin. The root of the word, *tvivl*, is the Danish word for "doubt." It corresponds to the German *Zweifel*. The prefix "*for-*" corresponds to the German prefix "*ver-*"; both serve to intensify the meaning of the root. Therefore, the Danish term *fortvivlelse*, like the German *verzweifeln*, means literally intensified doubt. Since doubting everything, even the possibility of significance and redemption, is to be without hope, it is correct to translate *fortvivlelse* as despair. However, the Danish term carries the connotation of intensified doubt in its etymology in a way that its English translation does not.

In order to understand Kierkegaard's use of *fortvivlelse*, it is important to understand the type of intensification of doubt involved. Doubt (*tvivl*) is a cognitive act. It occurs intellectually. The movement from doubt to despair, from *tvivl* to *fortvivlelse* is not made by a quantitative increase in one's cognitive powers. Rather, despair is an existential act. Kierkegaard has Judge William make this point when he writes "Doubt is a despair of thought, despair is a doubt of the personality" (*E/O* II, L215, H211). Later, the Judge writes "Doubt and despair therefore belong in entirely different spheres . . . Despair is precisely an expression for the whole personality, doubt only an expression for thought" (*E/O* II, L216, H212). Hence, understood etymologically, *fortvivlelse*, intensified doubt, is not to be taken as a quantitative increase in cognitive doubt. Rather, *fortvivlelse* is a doubt in one's personality that is not based on what is thought, but on what is lived. For this reason, "the lowliest, the least talented man, can despair" (*E/O* II, L217, H213).

In order to further understand Kierkegaard's use of the term *fortvivlelse*, it helps to analyze the concept *tvivl*. Like its English and German translations (doubt, *Zweifel*) the term is etymologically related to the number two. Just as in English there is an etymological connection between doubt and double, and in German there is a connection between *Zweifel* and *zwei*, there is a connection between the Danish *tvivl* and the concept "two," though it is not as obvious in Danish as it is in English or German.[3] With this clue, we can see that a doubt is a difference between two things, specifically between what one holds cognitively and what one is being asked to hold. Hence, in ordinary language we say "*I* doubt *that*," in such a way that we express that there is a gap between the two. With the concept *fortvivlelse*, this becomes a doubt of the personality. The doubling, the gap between two, is a gap within oneself. Hence, while Kierkegaard can use the term *fortvivlelse* to mean the same thing that we might ordinarily mean by the English word "despair," the Danish term more easily lends itself to an analysis of the self where there is a doubling in the self. In this way, we can more easily understand how Kierkegaard uses the term despair to refer both to the feeling of a loss of hope or significance and also to a misrelation in the self.

2. The Concept of Despair in Kierkegaard's Other Works

Kierkegaard discusses and explains the concept of despair more in *The Sickness Unto Death* than in all of his other published works together. Still, he does employ the term in other works and hence these uses deserve some attention.[4] Many of these uses of the term despair involve little or no analysis or explanation of the meaning of the concept. For example, in his dissertation, *The Concept of Irony*, Kierkegaard used the term despair three times without any special explanation. Other times, he devotes himself to clarifying the concept in his writing. In this way, the use of the concept of despair in writings other than *The Sickness Unto Death* can be divided into those usages of the term where there is no explanation of the meaning and those where there is. While I have listed the works in which all of the uses of the term *fortvivlelse* appear (see the preceding note), only those which include an explanation of the term merit attention.

Kierkegaard's first explanation of the concept of despair in a published work appears in *Either/Or Vol. II*, in the Judge's second letter. There, the Judge both describes the feeling of despair and explains that it is a misrelation in the self which gives rise to this feeling. The feeling of despair had been described first hand by the aesthete in *Vol. I*, but the Judge sums up these descriptions of the feeling of being in despair when he writes that for the aesthete all acts are

> done with as little teleology as possible . . . you take
> repose in despair, nothing concerns you, you will not get
> out of the way of anything, you say, 'If one were to throw
> a tile from the roof, I wouldn't get out of the way.' You
> are like a dying man, you die daily, not in the serious
> significance usually attached to this word, but life has
> lost its reality . . . You let everything pass you by, it makes
> no impression (*E/O* II, L200, H195-96).

Thus, the feeling of despair is the feeling of a loss of
significance. However, the Judge explains that this feeling is grounded in a misrelation in the self, specifically in
a failure to take responsibility for one's choices. The aesthete posits some condition outside of his control and
makes himself dependent upon that condition. In doing
so, he is "constantly beyond himself," that is, improperly
related to himself (*E/O* II, L199, H194). This misrelation is
termed despair.

In the *Concluding Unscientific Postscript*, the pseudonymous author Johannes Climacus explains the different notions of despair in volumes one and two of *Either/
Or*. Climacus explains that while "the first part was despair," this is different from the ethicist who "has despaired"
(*CUP*, L227, H I 253). The life of the aesthete is despair.
This differs from the ethicist who despairs willingly. The
ethicist chooses the self and in so doing recognizes the
impossibility of any finite thing being completely satisfactory. Hence, by choosing despair, he chooses himself rather
than a world of possibilities which give fleeting pleasure.

In *Fear and Trembling*, the pseudonymous author
Johannes de Silentio several times asks what might have
happened had Abraham despaired rather than had faith.[5]
However, *Fear and Trembling* contains only poetic speculation about the possibility of Abraham's despair; the work
does not include an analysis or clarification of the concept despair.

In *The Gospel of Suffering*, Kierkegaard briefly refers
to a different aspect of despair, in particular what he later

called the despair of defiance. He explains that one must learn from suffering. However, suffering is a hazardous kind of instruction, "for it may lead to defiance and despair" (*GS*, 54). Another brief reference to the despair of defiance is present in *Purity of Heart*, where Kierkegaard writes "Each rebel against God, in the last instance, is himself reduced to despair" (*PH*, 61). The despair of defiance is developed and explained more thoroughly in *The Sickness Unto Death*.

The theme of despair as a misrelation in the self appears in *Works of Love* in the context of a discussion of immediate love. Immediate love is a kind of desperation, though it may hide its desperation from itself. He writes "Despair is a disproportion in his [the one in immediate love] inmost being — so far down, so deep, that neither fate nor events can encroach upon it, but can only reveal the fact that the disproportion was there" (*WL*, 34).

Later in *Works of Love*, Kierkegaard uses the term despair to mean the abandonment of hope when he writes "Renouncing possibility is just what despair means" (*WL*, 205).

In *Training in Christianity*, Kierkegaard has the pseudonymous author Anti-Climacus use the existential difference between doubt and despair to explain the difference between disbelief and offense. Disbelief, like doubt, is a cognitive act. Offense, like despair, is an existential act. In *Training in Christianity*, Anti-Climacus argues that the proper relationship to Christ is either one of faith or one of offense. If, under the influence of modernity, one claims that one's relation to Christ is one of disbelief, then it shows a misunderstanding of the person of Christ. It reduces Christianity to a set of beliefs to be cognitively held rather than a relationship to an incarnate God which is to be existentially lived. Anti-Climacus uses the existential difference between doubt and despair to make this distinction.

Kierkegaard also uses the term despair in his journals. Several of these entries that discuss the relation between anxiety and despair will be discussed in chapter six. I will focus here on those entries which analyze or explain the concept of despair.

As early as 1836, Kierkegaard described his age as the age of despair (*SKJP* I, 737). In an entry in 1842, Kierkegaard discusses the despair of desiring death and stagnation and the relation of this kind of despair to the love of God. He writes

> When everything is lost, when that which to you is dearest of all is denied you, when there is not one remaining doubt which can keep the soul breathing, when it wants to sink down in stagnation and death "because there is nothing left to do"—could there really be absolutely nothing left? I do know of one thing still—before you lay yourself down to die, even though you keep on living, ask yourself: Do I still love God as deeply as before? (*SKJP* I, 742).

Hence, the view that Christian faith and the love of God is the cure for despair is already present six years before the writing of *The Sickness Unto Death*.

A number of the journal entries on despair have to do with Kierkegaard's father and reflections upon his despair (*SKJP* I, 740 & 745). These more autobiographical entries get developed later, so that by 1848, the entries in the journals that have to do with despair reflect the conceptual clarification of despair that is presented in *The Sickness Unto Death* (*SKJP* I, 747-50.). However, these few later entries on the meaning of despair for the most part duplicate or expand on material that is discussed in *The Sickness Unto Death*.

3. The Pseudonym: Anti-Climacus

In comparison to Vigilius Haufniensis, the pseudonym of *The Sickness Unto Death* is explained by Kierkegaard much more completely. To understand the pseudonym, it helps to reflect on some details of Kierkegaard's life. After publishing the *Postscript*, Kierkegaard had planned on taking a post as a country pastor and discontinuing his writing career. In the midst of deliberating about this next step in his career, he continued to write. During this time, four years after having published *The Concept of Anxiety*, he wrote *The Sickness Unto Death*. He was somewhat unsure of what he was going to do with the work, though he certainly considered publishing it under his own name.[6] Even the final copy of the title page that the publisher used contained several crucial changes. The subtitle was slightly altered and the author's name was changed three times. At first the author was listed as S. Kierkegaard. Then it was changed to Anticlimacus. Finally it was changed to Anti-Climacus. Kierkegaard's name was added to the title page as editor (*Pap.* VIII B 171:1-5 n.d., 1848).

In order to understand the meaning of the pseudonym, one must be familiar with another of Kierkegaard's pseudonyms: Johannes Climacus, i.e., John the Climber. Climacus is the pseudonymous author of two of Kierkegaard's published works, including his magnum opus, as well as one unpublished work.[7] Climacus, who is named after the 7th century ascetical theologian and author of *The Ladder of Divine Ascent*, is presented by Kierkegaard as being a young, intelligent man who seeks to come to know the truths of Christianity. Hence, he is a climber. Anti-Climacus is not opposed to Climacus. Rather, the prefix "anti-" is a version of "ante" meaning before, as in anticipate. It does not mean against (*SUD*, xxii). Nor is the name intended to sound anticlimactic. Rather, Anti-Climacus is the Christian at which Johannes Climacus was aiming.

The justification for the change to a pseudonym is given by Kierkegaard in his journals.

> It is absolutely right—a pseudonym had to be used. When the demands of ideality are to be presented at their maximum, then one must take extreme care not to be confused with them himself, as if he himself were the ideal. Protestations could be used to avoid this. But the only sure way is this redoubling. The difference from the earlier pseudonyms is simply but essentially this, that I do not retract the whole thing humorously but identify myself as one who is striving (*SKJP* 6, 6446).

Thus, Anti-Climacus is a higher pseudonym. His role is not like the lower pseudonyms, i.e., to point to the religious. Rather, Anti-Climacus is a religious author, so much so that Kierkegaard was humbled by the Christianity of Anti-Climacus. In this way, Kierkegaard maps his authorship, differentiating three distinct groups: the lower pseudonymous works whose role is to point to the religious sphere,[8] the upbuilding works that Kierkegaard signed, and the higher pseudonymous works.[9] "There is a stretch that is mine: the upbuilding; behind and ahead lie the lower and the higher pseudonymities; the upbuilding is mine, but not the aesthetic, not the pseudonymous works for upbuilding, either, and even less those for awakening" (*SKJP* 6, 6461). In this way, Anti-Climacus is not to be classed along with the lower pseudonyms.

In several journal entries, Kierkegaard distinguishes between Climacus and Anti-Climacus. "Climacus is lower, denies he is a Christian. Anti-Climacus is higher, a Christian on an extraordinarily high level" (*SKJP* 6, 6439).

> Johannes Climacus and Anti-Climacus have several things in common; but the difference is that whereas Johannes Climacus places himself so low that he even says himself that he is not a Christian, one seems to be able to detect in Anti-Climacus that he regards himself to be a Christian on an extraordinarily high level (*SKJP* 6, 6433).

Kierkegaard considers himself to be between Climacus and Anti-Climacus. "I would place myself higher than

Johannes Climacus, lower than Anti-Climacus" (*SKJP* 6, 6433). Still, the views that are presented by Anti-Climacus are views that Kierkegaard holds. The difference between Kierkegaard and Anti-Climacus is not a difference in what is cognitively held, but in what is existentially lived. Kierkegaard recognizes himself to be one still striving after an ideal that Anti-Climacus has come closer to achieving.

We get further insight into the character of Anti-Climacus through the epigraph and Preface of *The Sickness Unto Death*. The epigraph is a short prayer asking for eyes that see truth clearly. The Preface makes it clear that the work was written by a Christian scholar. Anti-Climacus uses a model of the Christian scholar that is apparently borrowed in part from Socrates's understanding of the philosopher in Plato's *Gorgias*. Just as Socrates understood the philosopher to be a doctor of the soul, Anti-Climacus writes that "everything essentially Christian must have in its presentation a resemblance to the way a physician speaks at the sickbed" (*SUD*, 5). The physician must be both a scientist and a healer. Using this model, Anti-Climacus acts as a scientist by observing and explaining the sickness in the self and as a healer by pointing to the redemptive act of Christ.

The Preface explains that the work is both scholarly and for Christian edification. Anti-Climacus confesses that the work may be too upbuilding to be completely scholarly, but defends himself against the charge that the book is too rigorous to be upbuilding. The book need not be intellectually accessible to everyone in order to retain an upbuilding intent. However, if a work is so scientific that in its scholarly indifference it lacks earnestness, then it is unethical and unchristian. Given the choice of being either edifying or scholarly, Anti-Climacus would prefer to be edifying. He explains that the correct existential response for a Christian to a discussion of despair and the self is earnestness. To seek a cognitive understanding without an earnest existential response is mistaken and unchristian. Anti-Climacus understands being a Christian to include, among other things, acting in such a way that everything is for edification, either for oneself or for others. In this way, Anti-Climacus shows himself to be an earnest concerned Christian despite his scholarly rigor, even in the prayer that begins the book and in the Preface.

4. *Psychology and Phenomenology in* The Sickness Unto Death

The subtitle of *The Sickness Unto Death* is "A Christian Psychological Exposition for Upbuilding and Awakening." In what sense is Anti-Climacus a psychologist? *The Sickness Unto Death* is like *The Concept of Anxiety* in that both have the word "psychological" (psychologisk) on the title page. In *The Concept of Anxiety*, Vigilius describes the science of psychology as having a rather limited domain. Vigilius writes

> The subject of which psychology treats must be something in repose that remains in a restless repose, not something restless that always either produces itself or is repressed. But this abiding something out of which sin constantly arises, not by necessity (for a becoming by necessity is a state) but by freedom—this abiding something, this predisposing presupposition, sin's real possibility, is a subject of interest for psychology. That which can be the concern of psychology and with which it can occupy itself is not that sin comes into existence, but how it can come into existence. Psychology can bring its concern to the point where it seems as if sin were there, but the next thing, that sin is there, is qualitatively different from the first. The manner in which this presupposition for scrupulous psychological contemplation and observation appears to be more and more comprehensive is the interest of psychology. Psychology may abandon itself, so to speak, to the disappointment that sin is there as an actuality. But this last disappointment reveals

the impotence of psychology and merely shows that its
service has come to an end (*CA*, 21-2).

Therefore, as Vigilius understands psychology, its proper
domain includes describing and providing a transcendental
explanation of psychological states. However, psychology is unable to give a causal account of sin, since sin is
a free act and free acts can not be causally explained.

Anti-Climacus is a psychologist in this sense, for he
describes the psychological state of despair. However, Anti-
Climacus understands despair before God to be sin. Hence,
his description of despair is sometimes a description of
sin. He is not, however, giving a causal explanation of
sin. Therefore, he has not violated Vigilius's distinction
between the domains of psychology and dogmatics even
though he gives psychological descriptions of sin.

The psychology of Anti-Climacus is one that is informed by Christian categories. The distinctions that are
made in his psychology and his phenomenological descriptions of despair are made in light of the Christian
category of sin. The book is divided into two parts. The
first part consists primarily of phenomenological descriptions of possible human forms of despair. The second
part explains that despair before God is sin. One might
be tempted to treat the first part as non-theological and
the second part as theological or dogmatic. However, this
interpretation would be flawed, for the distinctions that
are drawn in the first part are based on a religious view of
the self. Anti-Climacus is able to describe phenomenologically the possible forms of despair only because he is
developing what is already implied in his religious, Christian understanding of the self.

Anti-Climacus differs from Vigilius primarily in that
he is explicitly writing for edification. While both Vigilius
and Anti-Climacus take what might be called a basically
phenomenological approach to psychology, Vigilius limits
his work as a "simple psychologically orienting delibera-

tion." The Danish "*simpel*" is properly translated as simple, so long as we do not take this to connote easy or simple minded. Rather, it means a plain, merely psychologically orienting deliberation. In other words, Vigilius is simply giving a psychological description and conceptual clarification of anxiety; he points out that this conceptual clarification will provide insight into the dogmatic understanding of hereditary sin, but he does not write with the explicit direct goal of edifying the reader. On the other hand, Anti-Climacus subtitles his work "A Christian Psychological Exposition for Upbuilding and Awakening." He has the explicit immediate goal of awakening the reader in order that one may eradicate despair and sin in oneself through faith. This goal of edifying or building up the reader is a distinct yet related goal to describing and psychologically accounting for despair. The conceptual analysis of despair is a means to the goal of edification. *The Sickness Unto Death* differs from *The Concept of Anxiety* in that Anti-Climacus uses his conceptual clarification of despair in order to achieve his goal of edification; Vigilius points out that his conceptual clarification of anxiety can be used for edification, but he limits his project and does not include a section that aims at edification in his "simple psychological exposition." I will be focusing on Anti-Climacus's clarification of the concept of despair while keeping in mind that for Anti-Climacus, the analysis of despair is one that is informed by a religious view of the self and the analysis of despair is written with an explicitly Christian goal, namely that the reader may be awakened and edified, recognize sinfulness in oneself and seek to eradicate it, ultimately finding freedom through faith in Christ's redemptive grace.

With these introductory remarks, we are now able to turn to the text of *The Sickness Unto Death* in order to seek to clarify the concept of despair.

CHAPTER 5

Despair in *The Sickness Unto Death*

1. The Introduction: Death is not the Sickness

The introduction to *The Sickness Unto Death* makes it clear to the reader that Anti-Climacus is not writing simply as a scholar or as a psychologist, but as a Christian. This is evident both from the fact that the introduction begins with a quote from Scripture and from the following point.

Anti-Climacus begins with a line from the story of Lazarus in John's Gospel: "This sickness is not unto death." (John 11:4) "This" sickness, which Lazarus had, is death. The different reactions to Lazarus's death by Jesus and Lazarus's family indicate two views regarding the greatest malady in human life. Humanly speaking, death is the greatest evil. On this view, there is hope only as long as there is life. After Lazarus had died, Martha and Mary were upset. "If you had been here, he would not have died," Martha said to Jesus. This view, that death is the termination of life, has two aspects. On the one hand, it ignores the possibility of an afterlife. However, more importantly, it views death as the greatest problem in human life.

Anti-Climacus contrasts this view with Christ's, that is, with the view of Christianity. Christ stated clearly that

"Lazarus is dead".[1] But this sickness, death, was not the sickness unto death. Again, Christ's view has two aspects. First, death is not the end, for Christ taught that there is an afterlife. However, the point that Anti-Climacus is more concerned with making is that Christ, and thus Christianity, teaches that death is not the greatest evil in life. Neither are any of the things that may befall a person and are sometimes considered to be worse than death: torture, suffering, hardship, sickness, grief. Anti-Climacus implies but does not make explicit in the introduction that Christianity teaches that sin, or spiritual death, rather than physical death, is the greatest evil in human life.

Anti-Climacus explains in the introduction that this insight, that the sickness in the self is something other than the knowledge of one's mortality, comes only with Christian revelation and not simply through experience or self-reflection. "Only the Christian knows what is meant by the sickness unto death" (*SUD*, 8). He uses the metaphor of a child and an adult to make this point. "What makes the child shudder and shrink, the adult regards as nothing. The child does not know what the horrifying is; the adult knows and shrinks from it" (*SUD*, 8). The Christian does not fear pain, suffering, or physical death, for compared with the sickness unto death, these lesser dangers are like no danger at all.

2. The Opening Passage: The Self and Despair

The opening passage of *The Sickness Unto Death* is, at first reading, baffling, enigmatic, and Hegelian in the most pejorative sense.[2] It deserves special attention, since the rest of the book is to a great extent an expansion of the opening passage. Other scholars have sought to interpret this difficult passage, but none of the previous attempts have been completely satisfactory.[3] The previous analyses of *The Sickness Unto Death* have made it clear that for Kierkegaard the self is freedom. However, these scholars have not adequately shown that, as Louis Dupré has written, "The originality of Søren Kierkegaard's philosophy of the self lies not so much in the identification of the self with freedom, as in the fact that it relates this self-constituting freedom to a transcendent principle beyond freedom" (1963b, 506). Dupré does not focus primarily on the opening passage from *The Sickness Unto Death*. I will follow Dupré's view that for Kierkegaard a human being's relation to God is at the heart of the self and apply this interpretation rigorously to the entire opening passage from *The Sickness Unto Death*.

One of the first problems to face in interpreting this passage is the disparity in style between it and the rest of the book. The first passage is so algebraic, so abstract, so Hegelian, that I am sure many readers have put down the book immediately, perhaps never to pick it up again. But if one reads on, one notes a quick change in style. Most of the rest of the book is free of the self-consciously abstract formulations of the first section. Why the difference? In the opening passage, Anti-Climacus is poking fun at the abstract jargon of the Hegelians. Yet, at the very same time that he is mocking obtuse Hegelian formulas, he is using the abstract style to set forth his view of the self, a view that is crucially different from Hegel's.

In interpreting the meaning of the first section of *Sickness*, the section heading is often overlooked. Part one of the book, (the first 64 pages), is titled "The Sickness Unto Death is Despair." Section A of part one is titled "Despair is the Sickness Unto Death." Section A is broken into three parts. I will be focusing here on the perplexing part A.

Part A has a long title that gives valuable clues to understanding the text. The title reads:

> Despair is a sickness of the spirit, of the self, and accordingly can take three forms: in despair not to be conscious of having a self (not despair in the strict sense); in despair not to will to be oneself; in despair to will to be oneself (*SUD*, 13).

The chief clue in the section heading is the claim that despair can take three forms. Anti-Climacus tells us his goal is to offer an analysis of despair. Since despair is a sickness of the self, he must first offer an analysis of the self. Next, Anti-Climacus says that since despair is a sickness of the self, it can take three forms. This is related to the fact that the self can take three forms. Anyone familiar with Kierkegaard will recognize these as the aesthetic, the ethical and the religious. Therefore, when Anti-Climacus proceeds to offer an algebraic formula for the self, we should be warned that he is really offering three different formulas.

A line by line analysis of this passage is made difficult by the fact that Anti-Climacus does not neatly divide the three formulas for the self, though they are each presented. For the sake of clarity, I will divide these three structural formulas of the self, though keeping in mind that this division is simply a hermeneutical tool for understanding the text.

A. The Structure of the Aesthetic Self, or the Merely Human

The aesthete is a human being, but is not properly a self. In *Either/Or Vol. 2*, Judge William offers an analysis of the self of the aesthete. He writes "This self did not exist previously, for it came into existence by means of the choice, and yet it did exist, for it was in fact 'himself'" (*E/O* II, L219, H215). This is admittedly a difficult passage, but from the surrounding context we can tell that it means that the aesthete is only potentially a self. It is the ethical choice that makes the self an actual self. Thus, in the opening passage in *Sickness*, when Anti-Climacus discusses the human being who is not a self, he is referring to the aesthete, or at least to those who have not made the ethical choice.

A human being, as a mere human, is a synthesis of two poles. On the one side are aligned the physical, the finite, the temporal, and necessity. These all have to do with human facticity, as Anti-Climacus insists that an essential part of being human involves embodiment and having limits. Included in the other pole are the psychical, the infinite, the eternal, and freedom. These have to do with what is usually associated with the soul. They are primarily cognitive rather than volitional. The volitional element, individual choice, is absent in the mere human being. In this sense, the mere human being is not yet a self. The synthesis between these two poles, the physical and the psychical, in the mere human being is such that the relation is a negative unity. This means that the two poles are just there together. The connection between the two poles is inert. There is no dynamic interplay between the two. The individual is not responsible for the negative unity between the two. Hence, when one considers the mere human being, that is, one who has not made choices as an individual for which one is responsible, or to put it another way, when one considers the human being only under the qualification of the psychical, one sees that the human being is an inert relation.

The structural formula of the mere human being may be diagrammed as follows:

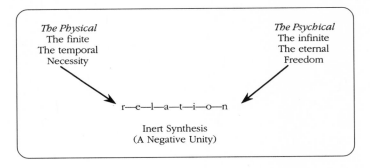

The Physical
The finite
The temporal
Necessity

The Psychical
The infinite
The eternal
Freedom

r—e—l—a—t—i—o—n

Inert Synthesis
(A Negative Unity)

This diagram represents the mere human being, which is a negative unity of opposite polarities. The relation is a negative unity inasmuch as it is inert. This relation, though it is inert, is a third thing apart from the two poles that it relates. This relation is not the self, that is, it does not take responsibility for its own choices and its own relation to itself; rather, it is the mere human being.

The diagram helps to explain Anti-Climacus's view of the structural formula of the mere human being, which he describes when he writes:

> A human being is a synthesis of the infinite and the finite, of the temporal and the eternal, of freedom and necessity, in short, a synthesis. A synthesis is a relation between two. Considered in this way, a human being is still not a self (*SUD*, 13).

This is the structural formulation for the human being who has not made choices as an individual for which he or she is responsible.

This structure forms the foundation of the next two structural formulations of the self. In the two remaining formulations, the poles do not change, only the nature of the relation changes. With this in mind, we proceed to the next structural formulation of the self.

B. The Structure of the Ethical Self

Anti-Climacus uses what is at first a complex formulation to describe the ethical choice. It may help if we recall Judge William's exhortation to the aesthete: choose yourself (*E/O* II, L215, H211, and elsewhere). The Judge describes how choosing oneself involves going out of one's self in order to become oneself. (*E/O* II, L255, H250-1). When a person chooses oneself, one relates oneself to oneself. This concept should not be so difficult to imagine, for we can imagine other self-reflexive activities: I talk to myself, I know myself. Anti-Climacus's self-reflexive term is "relating to oneself." When Anti-Climacus says that a person is able to relate oneself to oneself, he means two things: 1) that the person can be conscious of oneself, and 2) that the person can choose oneself. To say that a person is conscious of oneself is merely to say that the person is self-conscious and self-reflective. To say that a person can choose oneself is to say both that one has a nature and that one has a free will. Thus, to say that a person relates oneself to oneself is to say that the person is a self-conscious agent with a free will who can choose to fulfill one's nature.

We have seen in the first diagram that Anti-Climacus thinks that a mere human being is a relation. To add that this relation is a self-conscious agent with a free will is to say that the relation (the mere human being) relates oneself to oneself. This is what Anti-Climacus means when he writes "the relation relates itself to itself" (*SUD*, 13). When the relation (the person) relates oneself to oneself, the relating of oneself to oneself is a positive relation inasmuch as it is dynamic. The person oneself is responsible for this relating. It is not an inert relation, but an active one. Anti-Climacus writes "If the relation relates itself to itself, this relation is the positive third, and this is the self" (*SUD*, 13). This diagram may help.

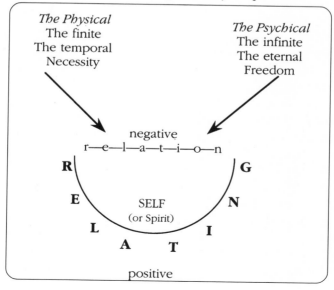

This diagram represents the self-established self, which is a *relation* (person) that relates itself to itself. There is a relation just by virtue of the fact that there is a person. Since this relation is inert, it is negative. When that person self-consciously and freely chooses himself or herself, then that person becomes a self. This is the relation's relating itself to itself. This relating is positive, since it is dynamic. The accent here is on an act of the will: the choosing of oneself. Again, Judge William's description of the ethical choice may help. He says that the self comes into existence by virtue of the ethical choice (*E/O* II, L217, H213). With this, the first few lines of the passage should begin to make sense.

> The self is a relation that relates itself to itself or is the relation's relating itself to itself in the relation; the self is not the relation, but is the relation's relating itself to itself (*SUD*, 13).

Using the diagram, it should be clearer what this means. To say that "The self is a relation that relates itself to itself" is the same thing as saying the self "is the relation's relating itself to itself in the relation." Both of these express the person's self-conscious act of choosing oneself. The act of choice is described in detail by Judge William in "Equilibrium" in *Either/Or, Vol. 2*. The act of choosing oneself is the act of producing oneself as a self.

If Anti-Climacus did not have a religious view of the self, the above description would be a complete description of what it means to be a self. For Judge William, the ethical choice to be oneself, to relate oneself to oneself, is what is central to the self. The Judge thinks that the self can attain a proper relation to God simply by "doing the best one can." The Judge admits that he is always falling short of the universal (*E/O* II, L334ff, H329ff, and elsewhere). However, his formula for overcoming this difficulty is to try harder. He does not recognize the existential necessity of faith in response to God's grace for establishing this relation. This is where the Judge and Anti-Climacus differ. Anti-Climacus agrees with Augustine when he writes in the *Confessions* "our heart is restless until it rests in

[God]" (1960, 43). On Anti-Climacus's view, the self comes into equilibrium only when it freely recognizes its dependence on God and relates itself to God in faith.

C. The Structure of the Religious Self

While the ethical self seeks to be in equilibrium solely by itself, the religious self finds equilibrium by relating itself to the power that established it as a human being. Anti-Climacus writes "Such a relation that relates itself to itself, a self, must either have established itself or have been established by another" (*SUD*, 13). The Judge thinks that the self established itself, and hence it could come into equilibrium on its own. Anti-Climacus disagrees. He holds that while the moment of ethical choice is necessary in order for there to be a self, the self did not create itself *ex nihilo*. Rather, the self produced itself out of a relation that was established by another. Moreover, the self can never properly relate itself to itself unless it relates itself to the power that established it.

The religious self can be diagrammed as follows.

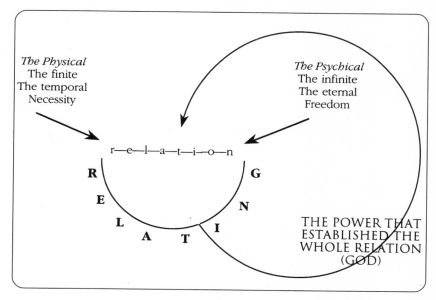

Anti-Climacus describes the structure of the religious self by writing:

> If the relation that relates itself to itself has been established by another, then the relation is indeed the third, but this relation, the third, is yet again a relation and relates itself to that which established the entire relation (*SUD*, 13).

In other words, since the self is a product of a relation that it did not itself establish, it must relate itself to that which did establish it. The self rightly relates itself to itself by rightly relating itself to the transcendent power which created it. Hence, Anti-Climacus's notion of the self as freedom is essentially religious. The self is freedom in the sense of right relation to oneself, to others, and to God. This kind of freedom is not merely procedural, as freedom of choice, but is substantive. Since the self is self-reflexive, social and religious, freedom is being oneself, that is taking responsibility for one's choices while living and acting in right relation to others and to God.

Having gotten this far in our examination of the opening passage from *Sickness*, the remainder of the passage is not nearly as difficult. The final point is to clarify the three kinds of despair.

Previously we examined the section heading. It began "Despair is a Sickness of the Spirit, of the Self, and accordingly can take three forms" (*SUD*, 13). I have shown that the three forms of despair are related to the fact that there are three kinds of selves. Though this is true, it may have been misleading. There is not a separate kind of despair that corresponds to each of the three structures of the self.

When Anti-Climacus uses the term despair here, he is not using it to describe a feeling or an affective state. To take him as doing so is to misunderstand his meaning. Of course, Kierkegaard does sometimes use the term despair to describe the feeling of a loss of significance.[4] Still, in this passage, despair has no affective connotations at all.

Rather, despair is a technical term used to describe a misrelation in the self (*SUD*, 14).

The religious structure of the self, where the self is a relation that relates itself to itself and in so doing relates itself to the power that established it, is the self in which all the parts of the self are properly related (*SUD*, 14). Since the third structural formation (the religious self) is the self without misrelation, and despair is a misrelation in the self, the third structural formulation is the self free from despair. Anti-Climacus calls this faith.

Now, this leaves us with three forms of despair but only two structural formulations for the self. This is no problem since the first kind of despair, not to be conscious of having a self, is not despair in the strict sense. This kind of despair applies to the first structural formulation of the mere human being. The self has not yet been posited because the person is not even conscious of having a self. In *Either/Or Vol. 2* Judge William distinguishes between six varieties of the aesthetic sphere of existence: 1) living for physical beauty, 2) living for wealth, honor, fame, one's beloved, 3) aiming at developing one's talents, 4) living for hedonistic pleasure, 5) living for self-reflective enjoyment, and 6) despair (*E/O* II, L185-202, H181-198). At the first five of the stages, or so the Judge seems to say, one is not conscious of being a self. Properly speaking, there is no misrelation in the self in these stages since there is no self. Therefore, Anti-Climacus calls this the despair of not being conscious of having a self, and he adds that this is not despair in the strict sense.

The sixth variety of the aesthetic sphere of existence that the Judge mentions is despair. At this stage, the aesthete is conscious of being a self, but he despairs of being a self. In other words, he does not choose to be a self. He consciously refuses to take responsibility for himself. In our passage from *Sickness*, Anti-Climacus calls this form of despair "not to will to be oneself" (*SUD*, 13). This kind of despair is just on the border of the first two structural formulations of the self. The person is conscious of being a self, but does not choose oneself. This sort of person does not take responsibility for himself or herself. Thus, the misrelation consists in a not willing to relate oneself to oneself. Anti-Climacus calls this first kind of despair (proper) the despair of not willing to be a self. Later in *Sickness*, he calls this the despair of weakness (*SUD*, 49ff).

The second kind of despair (proper) is in despair willing to be oneself. This is the despair of willing to be oneself on one's own, not in relation to the power that established the whole relation. Judge William is an example of this kind of despair. Judge William's fault is that he thought his willing to be a self was sufficient for an equilibrium of his personality. Sartre may be a perfect example of this kind of despair; he wants to be himself and at the same time deny that he is a creature (1956b, 289). There is a misrelation in one's self inasmuch as one thinks one can be a self without being a self in relation to God. Later in *Sickness*, Anti-Climacus calls this the despair of defiance (*SUD*, 67ff).

The opening passage, then, is a summary of the entire work. The goal of the book is to seek to understand despair so that one might arrive at faith and hence freedom. Despair is a misrelation in the self, a sickness for which we, as individuals, are responsible. It is a failure by an individual to be the being that one was created by God to be, namely a self-conscious agent responsible for one's own acts and yet dependent on God.

3. The Possibility and Actuality of Despair

Because a human being is a synthesis of the finite and the infinite which is able to relate itself to itself, the self is able to despair. Considered abstractly, the ability to despair, the possibility of misrelating oneself to oneself, is an excellence. Animals are unable to despair. Thus, "the possibility of this sickness is man's superiority over the animal" (*SUD*, 15). In this sense, the possibility of despair is an infinite advantage.

However, to be in despair, to have a misrelationship in one's self, is ruination (*SUD*, 15). In this way, the relationship between the possibility and actuality of despair are different from the possibility and actuality of most things. Usually, "if it is an excellence to be able to be this or that, then it is an even greater excellence to be that" (*SUD*, 15). However, despair is the misuse of possibility. A human being is able to despair since human beings are free. In order to be free, a human must have the power of "being able." Freedom, which entails the ability to imagine future possibilities and choose from among them, is the mark of the human's superiority over the animal. However, despair is a wrongful use of freedom. Therefore, to actualize the possibility of despair is not an excellence, but a failure.

Anti-Climacus does not dwell on the question of whether or not a human being is born in despair. He is not primarily interested in answering the question of whether or not despair is a possibility or an actuality in human infancy. However, this is an important question for my argument. The reason that Anti-Climacus does not dwell on the question is that he is writing to readers who are themselves in despair. His goal is for them to recognize their own despair and work to overcome it by faith and through grace. However, it is crucial to a proper understanding of despair to ask whether all human beings are actually in despair or if some (for example, very young children) have despair as a possibility though they are not actually in despair.[5]

There are several reasons to conclude that Anti-Climacus must hold that a human being is not born in despair. First, to claim that a human being is born in despair would deny human freedom. In order to make despair the responsibility of the individual, Anti-Climacus must claim that despair is the result of a free choice. Further, if a human being is born in despair, or if human beings despair of necessity, then the claim that the possibility of despair in humans is an excellence is unfounded. The reason that the possibility of despair is an excellence is because it shows that human beings are free. Hence, in order for there to be human freedom, despair must be a possibility for a human being at the beginning of one's life, but it cannot be an actuality. Second, though Anti-Climacus does not take up the question of whether infants are in despair, he does make it clear that despair is not a flaw in the human being with which one is born. He writes:

> Despair is the misrelation in the relation of a synthesis that relates itself to itself. But the synthesis is not the misrelation; it is merely the possibility, or in the synthesis lies the possibility of the misrelation. If the synthesis were the misrelation, then despair would not exist at all, then despair would be something that lies in human nature as such (*SUD*, 15-6).

Despair is a sickness in the self that is brought about through one's own wrongful use of freedom. Anti-Climacus writes "Is [despair] something that happens to a person? No, it is his own fault" (*SUD*, 102). Since despair is not a flaw in human nature, it cannot be something with which human beings are born. Thus, human beings are born with the possibility of despair. The actuality of despair is the ruination of oneself that is brought about through one's wrongful use of freedom.

The relationship between the possibility and actuality of despair is different from the usual relationship between possibility and actuality on one further point. Usually, once a possibility has been actualized, it continues as a matter of course. For example, once a seed becomes a tree, it remains a tree. However, once a person is in despair, the despair does not necessarily continue as a matter of course. Rather, "every actual moment of despair is traceable to possibility; every moment he is in despair he is bringing it upon himself" (*SUD*, 17). Since despair is a misrelation in the self, and the self is a relation which relates itself to itself, despair can not be attributed to the misrelation, but to the relation which relates itself to itself. Thus, no moment of actual despair necessitates its continuation as despair. Rather, if despair continues, it is because the possibility of despair remains and the self continues to misrelate itself to itself.

4. Despair is "The Sickness Unto Death"

One might expect that Kierkegaard would have titled this book "The Concept of Despair." In many ways, it is a conceptual clarification of the concept of despair in the same way that *The Concept of Anxiety* is a clarification of the concept of anxiety. However, as we have already seen, *The Sickness Unto Death* is not written simply in order to clarify a concept, but also to awaken and upbuild. For this reason, the book sometimes seeks to clarify the concept of despair while at other times the writing focuses on the existential aspect of despair with the goal of awakening the reader to self-analysis. The short section titled "Despair is 'The Sickness Unto Death'" has a more existential tone than the preceding sections.

The concept of the sickness unto death does not refer to a physical sickness. Anti-Climacus writes as a Christian, and hence he does not take death to be the absolute end of life; rather, "Christianly understood, death is a passing into life" (*SUD*, 17). The sickness unto death is a sickness that is not even cured by physical death. When one is physically ill, one turns away from death and hopes for life. When one is terminally ill and in great pain, one hopes for death, for when one dies, the sickness is over.

The sickness unto death that Anti-Climacus describes is a sickness that is not even cured through physical death. "When the danger becomes so great that death becomes the hope, then despair is the hopelessness of not even being able to die" (*SUD*, 17).[6]

Despair is the sickness unto death, for despair is an impotent self-consuming. Despair, which is a willed misrelation to oneself, is an attempt to do away with oneself. However, since the self has an aspect that is eternal, it can never completely succeed. "If a person were to die of despair as one dies of a sickness, then the eternal in him, the self, must be able to die in the same sense as the body dies of sickness. But this is impossible; the dying of despair continually converts itself into a living" (*SUD*, 17). Thus, despair is an attempt to do away with oneself, either by fleeing from oneself or by defiantly attempting to be a self that one is not. The attempt to do away with oneself is a sickness. Since Christianly understood, physical death is not the end of life, despair is the sickness unto death in the sense that it is the impotent attempt to do away with the self. Despair is the torment of trying to do away with oneself without ever being able to succeed. Hence, despair is the sickness unto death.

There is a difference between despairing over something and despairing over oneself. Anti-Climacus distinguishes between the common understanding and the expert's understanding of despair. The common understanding of despair is that when a person is in despair, the person is in despair about a particular situation. When a situation works out differently from what one had hoped and when there is no hope of rendering the situation, we say the person is in despair. However, Anti-Climacus claims that this despair over something is merely a symptom and not the true despair. He uses the example of a young girl whose beloved has died. She despairs over the situation, for there is no longer any hope of her being with her beloved.

Yet this is not the primary sense in which Anti-Climacus uses the term despair. The despair over this situation is grounded in a despair over herself. The young girl does not want to be herself. This self becomes a torment to her if she has to be a self without him (*SUD*, 20). She wants to be a self which she cannot be. This attempt to be something other than oneself, this misrelation in the self, is the despair over oneself. Just as the doctor is more concerned with the illness than with its symptoms, Anti-Climacus is more concerned with despair over oneself, which is the illness, than despair over some thing or situation, which is merely a symptom of a misrelation in the self.

The despair with which Anti-Climacus is concerned is the despair over oneself, the impotent attempt to be rid of oneself. Since the self is eternal, the attempt to be rid of oneself is continuously a failed project. Eternity will "nail him to himself so that his torment will still be that he cannot rid himself of his self, and it will become obvious that he was just imagining that he had succeeded in doing so" (*SUD*, 21). Therefore, the despair over oneself is the sickness unto death.

5. The "Universality" of Despair

Since this work is written to awaken and upbuild, Anti-Climacus's main goal is to bring the reader to the point of recognizing his or her own despair and to seek a cure in Christian faith. In an effort to awaken the reader to recognize his or her own despair, Anti-Climacus writes that this sickness, despair, is "universal." One might be tempted to interpret this to mean that despair is essential to human being such that so long as one is human, one is in despair. However, this is not Anti-Climacus's meaning.

The Danish term that is here translated as "universality" is *almindelighed*. While the root *almin* can mean universal, it can also mean general or common. So too, while the term *almindelighed* can be interpreted to mean universality, it can also mean that which is generally valid. In English, there is a clear difference between saying that something is common and saying that something is universal. That which is universal is essential to a thing, while that which is common is not necessarily essential. I will show that Anti-Climacus cannot mean that despair is literally universal. Rather, in saying that it is *almindeligbed*, he means that it is much more widespread and common than we had previously thought.

In the preceding section, Anti-Climacus had made it clear that the possibility of despair is essential to human being while the actualization of despair is the responsibility of the individual and is due to the self's wrongful use of freedom. It would follow from this that, for example, very young children who have not yet made any free choices are not yet actually in despair. Also, since Anti-Climacus claims that the opposite of despair is faith, he claims that the true Christian is not in despair (*SUD*, 22). This would be another example of a human being who is not in despair. Finally, though Anti-Climacus does not take up the question of Christology in this section, he would have to claim that Jesus Christ was both human and not in despair.[7] This too would be an example of a human being who is not in despair. Hence, there are at least three examples of human beings who are not in despair: infants, true Christians and the person Jesus Christ. Therefore, when Anti-Climacus writes that despair is "universal," he does not mean that it is essential to human being to be actually in despair.

Rather, the claim that despair is "universal" is an overstatement used with a rhetorical purpose, namely to encourage the reader to reflect upon his or her own despair and recognize despair where it had previously been ignored. Hence, the claim that despair is *almindeligbed* (universal, common) is a rhetorical claim that despair is far more pervasive than one might have realized. However, to be consistent, the most that Anti-Climacus can claim is that all who have misused freedom are actually in despair. He cannot claim that all human beings are in despair and that despair is essential to being human, else despair would not be the fault of the individual. Therefore, the "universality" of despair is simply that those who have wrongly used freedom are in despair, and that this includes far more people than one might at first expect.[8]

The main reason that Anti-Climacus claims despair is more widespread than we commonly think is because the common view fails to distinguish between the symptom and the cause of despair. The common view uses the term despair to denote the feeling of despair or the despair over something. However, as Anti-Climacus showed in the preceding section, these are merely symptoms that are grounded in the willful attempt to be something other than oneself.

Just as the physician distinguishes between the symptom and the cause of a sickness, Anti-Climacus distinguishes between the symptoms and the cause of despair (*SUD*, 23). The physician is more interested in the cause of a disease than in the symptoms. A person who is ill may not be aware of the illness until the symptoms have surfaced. By the time the symptoms have surfaced and exhibited themselves, the disease is sometimes quite advanced. Thus, the physician must look primarily at the disease itself, and hence the reported health of the individual may be merely the appearance of health. In an analogous way, the physician of the self is more concerned with whether or not the self is rightly related to itself than in the individual's reports of the feeling or lack of feeling of despair (*SUD*, 23).

Anti-Climacus claims that it is very common for individuals to be in despair, that is, to have a misrelation in oneself, without being conscious of it, that is, without feeling despair. In fact, Anti-Climacus claims that the most common form of despair is not to be conscious that one is in despair. This form of despair is discussed and explained in the next section. It is important here because it further explains the sense in which despair is "universal." Despair is "universal," that is, much more widespread than the common view considers it to be, because not to be conscious that one is misrelated to oneself is a widespread form of despair. In writing this, Anti-Climacus hopes to awaken the reader to earnest self-reflection and to recognize a misrelation in one's self where there is such a misrelation.

Since one may seek a cure for despair if one recognizes that one is in despair but will not if one is in despair but does not recognize it, Anti-Climacus is trying to induce the symptoms of despair to exhibit themselves in the individual. Through feeling despair, one can come to recognize that one is in despair. One can then learn that the feeling of despair is a symptom caused by a misrelation in the self that preceded the feeling. Through recognizing the sickness, one can seek a cure. In this way, though feeling despair is undesirable, it is better to feel despair and seek a cure than to be free of the feeling of despair and still have a misrelation in oneself of which one is unaware. Since the undesirable feeling of despair has the benefit of inducing the individual to seek a cure for the misrelation in the self, Anti-Climacus writes that despair is "universal," that is, much more widespread than commonly thought, in the hopes of making the reader feel despair, recognize that this is grounded in a misrelation in the self, and then seek the cure of Christian faith.

6. The Forms of Despair

In the last and longest section of the first part of the book, Anti-Climacus describes and gives an account of the various forms of despair. There are five main forms of despair that Anti-Climacus describes in this section.

The first form of despair is the despair of infinitude and possibility. Anti-Climacus discusses this form of despair in two sections, but both are essentially the same.[9] To understand this form of despair, one may either describe it poetically or define it dialectically. Anti-Climacus is more interested in giving an account of despair, and hence he defines this form of despair dialectically, that is, in relation to its opposite. In this way, the despair of infinitude is to lack finitude. Since a human being is a synthesis of two poles, of both the physical and the psychical, of both finitude and infinitude, of both possibility and necessity, to overemphasize one pole to the neglect of the other is to have a misrelation in oneself. Thus, every human existence that "simply wants to be infinite is despair" (*SUD*, 30). Since a human being is in part finite and hence has necessary limits, to neglect one's necessary finitude is to have a misrelation in one's self.

The despair of infinitude and possibility can be described as a poetic form of existence where one lives in fantasy and the imagination. Those romantics who sought to escape the mundane world of facticity through imagination and attempted to live a life of limitless possibility are examples of the despair of infinitude. So too, the Hegelian longing to know and understand the world from an infinite number of perspectives simultaneously, to gain the vantage point of absolute spirit, is an example of the despair of infinitude. The despair of infinitude is phenomenologically and poetically described by Kierkegaard in a number of places in the aesthetic literature. For example, the aesthete in volume one of *Either/Or*[10] and the character of the young man in "In Vino Veritas" in *Stages on Life's Way*[11] are characters who portray the despair of infinitude. These examples of the despair of infinitude each show a lack of finitude in the person. Such forms of existence ignore human facticity. For, as Judge William writes, to be a self means to be "an individual who has these [particular] passions, these inclinations, these habits, who is under these influences" (*E/O* II, L266-7, H262). Being human entails particularity, facticity, and limitedness. To ignore this, either through an overemphasis of the imagination or of abstract reason, is to be in the despair of infinitude and possibility.

The second form of despair is the despair of finitude and necessity. Again, Anti-Climacus discusses this form of despair in two essentially similar sections.[12] Like the despair of infinitude and possibility, the despair of finitude and necessity must be defined dialectically in terms of its opposite. The despair of finitude and necessity is the lack of infinitude and possibility. This form of despair is the misrelation in the self that comes about by being so bound up in the finite and the necessary, in the mundane narrowness of everyday life, that there is a neglect of the infinite and the possible. The despair of finitude and necessity is the complete lack of imagination such that one never acts on one's own and takes a risk. It is to cut oneself off from the possibility of breaking out of the mundane.

The despair of finitude and necessity can be described as a mundane form of existence where one does what is expected without ever thinking about the possibility of anything new. Here, the individual abandons his or her individuality to the crowd, the mass. This form of existence has the advantage of being momentarily comfortable, for so long as one never ventures anything new, one never experiences particular defeats. Indeed, so far as appearances go, this form of existence is respectable to the crowd. Still, since a human being is a synthesis of the finite and the infinite, of the necessary and the possible, to live only in finitude, only in necessity, is to have a misrelation in the self. This form of despair is exemplified in determinism and fatalism. Both determinism and fatalism fail to recognize that human beings have the power of imagination and the ability to act upon novel possibilities. Finally, the despair of finitude and necessity is important for Christianity, since Christianity claims that all things are possible with God. The despair of finitude and necessity is a denial that for God all things are possible.

The third form of despair is ignorance that one is in despair, or ignorance that one is a self. In order for Anti-Climacus to be consistent, it is necessary to assume that he is making a distinction that he does not explain. There is a traditional scholastic distinction between two kinds of ignorance: vincible and invincible ignorance. Invincible ignorance is ignorance for which one is not responsible. On the other hand, when one is vincibly ignorant, then one lacks knowledge that one should be expected to have. For example, if a person violates a written contract that the person had signed because the document was not read, then the person is vincibly ignorant, for though the person did lack knowledge, the person is responsible for the ignorance due to negligence. When Anti-Climacus refers to ignorance, he refers to vincible ignorance, that is, ignorance for which the individual is responsible. Since despair is a misrelation in the self for which the agent is responsible, the despair of not knowing that one is a self can only be despair for those who are vincibly ignorant.

Anti-Climacus does not clarify who is and is not vincibly ignorant. Instead, he assumes that anyone who is able to read the book would be vincibly ignorant if ignorant that the task of human life is to be a self. However, it is legitimate to ask if there is anyone who might reasonably not know that the task of a human life is to be an individual self. We can look at two extreme cases. It seems clear that infants should not be expected to know that they are to be selves. Hence, they are not in despair. On the other hand, Anti-Climacus assumes that anyone who could read his book, or perhaps any normal adult in

Christendom, should know that to be a human being means having the task of being a self. Infants should not be expected to know that they are to be selves. Those who are somewhere between the level of understanding of an infant and that of a normal adult are in despair only to the extent that they should know that they are to be selves and yet have kept themselves ignorant. This would include older children and people who are mentally handicapped. Ultimately, because of Anti-Climacus's self-reflective method, the only one who can determine if one is vincibly ignorant that one is a self is oneself.

Anti-Climacus explains that people delude themselves to keep themselves ignorant that the task of human life is to be a self. He uses the metaphor of a house to explain his meaning.

> Imagine a house with a basement, first floor, and second floor planned so that there is or is supposed to be a social distinction between the occupants according to floor. Now, if what it means to be a human being is compared with such a house, then all too regrettably the sad and ludicrous truth about the majority of people is that in their own house they prefer to live in the basement. Every human being is a psychical-physical synthesis intended to be spirit; this is the building, but he prefers to live in the basement, that is, in the sensate categories (*SUD*, 43).

To be vincibly ignorant that one is to be a self is to be in despair, for it is a failure to be oneself. If one does not know that it is one's task to be a self, to be a self-conscious agent responsible for one's acts and yet dependent on God, then one can not be a self. Anti-Climacus claims that most people who should know that the task of a human life is to be a self prefer to delude themselves and remain unaware of their task by remaining in sensate categories. This is the despair of being unaware that one is in despair since one is unaware that one is a self.[13]

The fourth form of despair is despair in weakness. There are a number of ways in which the despair in weakness can occur, but all share one thing in common. The despair in weakness is a misrelation in the self which is brought about by not willing to be oneself. It is not the direct result of an action by the person. Rather, it is the result of a failure to will to be oneself, and hence is despair in weakness.

The first way that one may not will to be oneself is to live a life of immediacy (*SUD*, 51). The person who lives a life of immediacy posits some condition outside of his or her control and assumes that living for the fulfillment of that condition will bring meaning and satisfaction to one's life. Examples of living a life of immediacy include living for health, physical beauty, money, honor, fame, one's beloved, or pleasure. The person who lives this type of life only experiences despair when some event occurs that is different from what is expected and that is thought to be the ruin of one's life. For example, if a person lives a life of immediacy for one's beloved and then the beloved unexpectedly dies, the person may be thrown into despair. However, Anti-Climacus explains that from the point of view of the physician of the soul, the despair preceded the melancholy state into which the person was thrust. The despair is the misrelation in the self. The person in immediacy does not live as a self-conscious agent responsible for his or her own acts. Instead, the person's acts are responses to the condition that is outside of the person's control. By being controlled by some condition outside of the control of the individual, the person is not willing to be a self. In this way, the despair over something earthly is a symptom of not willing to be oneself.

The next type of despair in weakness is that of the person in immediacy but with some reflection (*SUD*, 54). Here, the person is still in immediacy, that is, has posited some condition outside of his or her control the fulfillment of which is assumed to bring satisfaction. However, this person is more reflective. Through reflection, the person plays out in imagination a possibility and sees the meaningless of living a life based on some condition that is not in his or her control. Thus, the person despairs. The difference between this kind of despair and the previous despair is that here, the feeling of despair is brought about through the person's own reflection whereas in the previous case, the feeling of despair was brought about by some unexpected blow. However, in both cases, the feeling of despair is merely a symptom of a misrelation in the self where the person fails to will to be a self.

The youth's despair is another type of the despair of weakness (*SUD*, 58-9). The youth's despair is to long for some future condition, to hope for something yet to come and to live in that hope. This longing for the future, the illusion of hope, is really a failure to be oneself by not willing to be oneself. The reverse side of this is the adult's despair, which is a longing for the past and is yet another type of despair of weakness (*SUD*, 58-9). This longing for the past, the illusion of recollection, is a double delusion of oneself. First, in recalling the past, one tends to poeticize it by remembering only what one wants to remember. Second, and more importantly, by living in the past, one is failing to be oneself, for the past is no longer present. In this way, the adult's despair, like the youth's despair, is a misrelation in the self that is a not willing to be oneself.

So far, all of the types of the despair in weakness have been a despair over something earthly, some finite thing. One has something tragic and unexpected happen, and hence despairs, or imagines that something tragic and unexpected could happen at any time, or longs only for the future, or only for the past, and in each case some particular thing brings about the feeling of despair which is a symptom of some prior misrelation in the self. The next type of despair of weakness is the despair over everything earthly (*SUD*, 60). For if one despairs over one particular finite thing, one may soothe the feeling of despair by positing some different condition, still outside of one's control, that is assumed to bring satisfaction. The lover whose beloved dies may become attracted to a new beloved, or may begin to live for money. However, through reflection, one may see that no finite thing which is outside of one's control can satisfy the self. This despairing over the earthly and the possibility of any finite thing to bring satisfaction is an important step in self-consciousness that leads to the next type of despair in weakness.

Having recognized that something earthly and finite cannot bring satisfaction to the self, the self may nonetheless remain in despair. The self may now recognize itself as having been in despair and make a turn to faith. However, another option remains. "Instead of definitely turning away from despair to faith and humbling himself under his weakness, he entrenches himself in despair and despairs over his weakness" (*SUD*, 61). In this way, the despair over something earthly, or the despair over the earthly, may become the despair over oneself.

Anti-Climacus distinguishes between the "despair over" and the "despair of" something. One "despairs over" that which binds one in despair, for example, "over a misfortune, over the earthly, over a capital loss" (*SUD*, 60-1). However, one "despairs of" that which has the ability to release one from despair, for example, "of the eternal, of salvation, of one's own power" (*SUD*, 61). Since the self is sometimes what binds one in certain kinds of despair and other times what may release one from other kinds of despair, it is possible to discuss either the "despair over" or the "despair of" oneself.

We saw above that the despair over something earthly may become despair over oneself if, after having recognized the inability of any finite thing to bring satisfaction one refuses to make a definite turn to faith. In this way, despair over something may become despair over oneself. But despair over oneself is really a despair of the eternal. Through reflection, the person gained a vague consciousness of oneself as a self. In despairing over the earthly and the possibility of any finite thing to satisfy oneself, the person comes to see that no finite thing can satiate the self because the self is in part infinite and eternal. When the person then despairs over oneself, one has already come to see the self as eternal, and hence to despair over oneself is to despair of the eternal.

Anti-Climacus describes the way that the person despairs over himself or herself as closing oneself up within oneself, that is, of inclosing reserve (*SUD*, 63). We have already seen that the concept of inclosing reserve has been used by Vigilius Haufniensis in *The Concept of Anxiety*.[14] Vigilius explained that inclosing reserve is the turning in on oneself and shutting oneself off from something. However, Vigilius described the type of inclosing reserve where one shuts oneself off from the good, namely, redemption. This type of inclosing reserve is discussed and explained by Anti-Climacus in the following section (*SUD*, 67-74). The type of inclosing reserve that Anti-Climacus presents in this section is less severe. The person in this type of despair has closed oneself off from oneself, but remains in one's normal relations with the rest of the world. "He is a university graduate, husband, father, even an exceptionally competent public office holder, a respectable father, pleasant company, very gentle to his wife, solicitude personified to his children" (*SUD*, 64). He busies himself with his social relations and obligations, but all the time is evading himself. He has closed himself off from himself; he is not willing to be himself. Hence, this inclosing reserve is a type of the despair of weakness, since it is a not willing to be oneself. The mark of every type of the despair of weakness is that it is an evasion of oneself and a not willing to be oneself.

The fifth and final form of despair that Anti-Climacus describes in part one is the despair of defiance. In this form of despair, the individual is conscious of being a self. Further, the individual wills to be a self. However, in this form of despair, the individual insists on being a self alone and on one's own. This self defiantly rejects dependence on God. When this defiant willing to be oneself becomes intensified, the person turns in upon oneself and rejects any help from God. This is a kind of inclosing reserve, but it is different from the type explained above. Now the individual is not primarily closing oneself off from oneself, but from God. Yet, since to be a self means to be a creature dependent on God, to insist on being an independent self is in a sense a not willing to be oneself. When this form of despair is intensified, the person closes up within oneself and refuses to be related to God. This type of inclosing reserve, as Vigilius had explained, is the demonic (*SUD*, 73). In this form of despair, the individual defiantly wills to be a self while refusing to be dependent on God.

> Figuratively speaking, it is as if an error slipped into an author's writing and the error became conscious of itself as an error . . . and now this error wants to mutiny against the author, out of hatred toward him, forbidding him to correct it and in maniacal defiance saying to him: No, I refuse to be erased; I will stand as a witness against you, a witness that you are a second-rate author (*SUD*, 74).

7. Despair Before God: Sin

Part two of *The Sickness Unto Death* is more explicitly religious than part one. Having completed the conceptual clarification and phenomenological descriptions of despair in part one, Anti-Climacus turns to an explicitly religious analysis of despair in part two and in particular to an analysis of the meaning of sin. His goal in this part, as throughout the book, is to bring the reader to recognize his or her own sinfulness and hence turn to aid from grace through faith. Much of the content of the second part is an analysis of the meaning of sin, not of despair. It is possible to understand Anti-Climacus's concept of despair without a full analysis of part two of *The Sickness Unto Death*. In part two, Anti-Climacus explains that sin is despair before God. However, since his concept of sin is parasitic upon his concept of despair, it is not possible to understand Anti-Climacas's concept of sin without the analysis of the concept of despair presented in part one of his book.

In defining sin, Anti-Climacus extends his account of despair by emphasizing that sin is despair before God, or with the conception of God. Like despair, sin is a willed misrelation in the self. When one focuses on the relationship to God, despair, the willed misrelation in the self, is also a misrelationship with God. Anti-Climacus explains the relationship between sin and despair when he writes

> Sin is: before God, or with the conception of God, in despair not to will to be oneself, or in despair to will to be oneself. Thus sin is intensified weakness or intensified defiance: sin is the intensification of despair. The emphasis is on before God, or with a conception of God; it is the conception of God that makes sin dialectically, ethically, and religiously what lawyers call "aggravated" despair (*SUD*, 77).

To say that one despairs "before God" means that one has a conception of a transcendent, personal God (*SUD*, 81). When one either fails to take responsibility for oneself or attempts to be oneself without admitting one's dependence on God and does either with a conception of a transcendent personal God, then one's despair is sin (*SUD*, 81).

To seek to understand sin merely through an enumeration of specific sins, that is, to give examples of sins, is not an adequate understanding of sin. Instead, Anti-Climacus gives a general definition of sin that includes every specific example of sin. Anti-Climacus claims that murder, stealing, and fornication are instances of despairing before God since each are a self-willfulness against God. "Therefore, the definition embraces every imaginable and every actual form of sin" (*SUD*, 82). In this way, according to Anti-Climacus, every sin is despair before God.

Anti-Climacus makes it clear that his conception of sin is different from that of Socrates. Socrates held that sin is ignorance. He assumed that no one could knowingly do evil. Anti-Climacus claims that in the Christian conception of sin, the act of the will is central. Anti-Climacus agrees with Socrates that ignorance is sin, but only insofar as one is willfully ignorant. Further, Anti-Climacus claims that one may willfully do evil with knowledge. "Therefore, interpreted Christianly, sin has its roots in willing, not in knowing" (*SUD*, 95).

The second part of part two is a description of three types of sin: the sin of despairing over one's sin, the sin of despairing of the forgiveness of sins, and the sin of dismissing Christianity as untruth (*SUD*, 109-31). Here, Anti-Climacus shows particular ways in which one may sin.

Anti-Climacus claims that by faith it is possible to eradicate the self of despair before God, that is, it is possible to be redeemed of sin. Sin is despair before God, that is, either in weakness failing to be oneself or in defiance attempting to be a self independent of God. The formula for the self where despair has been overcome is "in relating itself to itself and in willing to be itself, the self rests transparently in the power that established it" (*SUD*, 131). Anti-Climacus claims that, having wrongfully used freedom, that is, having despaired, the self is unable to bring itself into equilibrium. The self can only be free from despair before God, that is, absolved from sin, through Christ's redemption. Therefore, the formula for the self that has overcome despair is also the formula for faith (*SUD*, 131).

Earlier, I argued that Vigilius Haufniensis's treatment of the relationship between anxiety and sin was incomplete since he had not explained the concept of sin.[15] Here, in the second part of *The Sickness Unto Death*, Anti-Climacus explains that sin is despair before God. Therefore, the relationship between anxiety and sin entails the relationship between anxiety and despair. Having set forth Kierkegaard's conception of despair as it is presented by Anti-Climacus in *The Sickness Unto Death*, it is possible to take the next step where I will make explicit the relationship between anxiety and despair in the thought of Kierkegaard.

CHAPTER 6
Drawing Out the Relationship Between Anxiety and Despair in Kierkegaard's Writings

T he relationship between anxiety and despair in
Kierkegaard's thought is central for several key
topics. First, this is where we find the connection
between freedom and its misuses. Philosophically, this is
the key to understanding Kierkegaard's contribution to a
fuller understanding of human freedom. Theologically,
the relationship between anxiety and despair is central to
comprehending Kierkegaard's interpretation of the relationship between original sin and sin. Psychologically,
this is where Kierkegaard's ideas on the connection
between environmental conditioning and personal responsibility are buried. And embedded in what he has to say
about the relationship between anxiety and despair, we
will find social and political insights that may help us
rethink the meaning of freedom in the age of anxiety.

However, Kierkegaard's ideas on the relationship between anxiety and despair are hidden, awaiting explication. Rarely does he examine the precise connection
between them. So although Kierkegaard has laid out the
structure of each, interpretive work remains if we are to
understand the relationship between anxiety and despair.

1. The Relationship in The Concept of Anxiety

The Concept of Anxiety was written four years before *The Sickness Unto Death*. It is not clear to what extent Kierkegaard had thought through his views on despair and sin at the time that *The Concept of Anxiety* was written. Kierkegaard had already had Judge William in *Either/Or Vol. 2* discuss the concept of despair. Further, though Judge William's analysis of despair is not as thorough as the later analysis offered by Anti-Climacus, Judge William's explanation of the term does not contradict the more complete analysis offered in *The Sickness Unto Death*.

There is virtually no explanation of the concept of despair by Vigilius in *The Concept of Anxiety*. In particular, Vigilius does not explain the concept of sin in terms of despair. It is unclear how much of this is due to the way that Vigilius approaches his topic and how much of this is due to Kierkegaard. It is possible that in 1844, Kierkegaard was not yet clear on the concept of sin and his later claim in *The Sickness Unto Death* that sin is despair before God.

The term despair (*fortvivlelse*) is only used 6 times in *The Concept of Anxiety* (*CA*, 105, 107, 115, 116, 131, 135). Further, Vigilius does not explain the sense in which he uses the term. The few times that the term despair is used in *The Concept of Anxiety*, it denotes the feeling of a loss of significance. Vigilius does not use the term in the technical sense that is developed in *The Sickness Unto Death* where despair is a misrelation in the self. Since the concept of despair is not explained in *The Concept of Anxiety*, there is also no explicit explanation of the relationship between anxiety and despair.

Instead, if we are to examine the relationship between anxiety and despair in *The Concept of Anxiety*, we will have to look at the relationship between anxiety and sin.

This interpretive problem is complicated by the fact that Vigilius explicitly refuses to give a conceptual analysis of sin. He claims to be using solely a psychological method. Since sin is a dogmatic concept that can only be fully understood with revelation, the methods of psychology alone are inadequate for an understanding of sin. Vigilius discusses the relationship between anxiety and sin but never explains what he means by sin.

However, in *The Sickness Unto Death*, Anti-Climacus does give a conceptual analysis of sin. We have seen that he avoids Vigilius's criticism of using a psychological method to analyze a dogmatic concept by using a psychology that is explicitly informed by Christian categories. With this difference, Anti-Climacus is able to clarify the concept of sin using Christian psychology. As we have seen, he explains sin to be despair before God.

Hence, if Anti-Climacus were to explain the relationship between anxiety and despair using Vigilius's analysis of anxiety, he would focus on the relationship between anxiety and sin. Vigilius explains that anxiety is the condition for the possibility of the first sin. Anti-Climacus explains that sin is despair before God. Therefore, the original relationship between anxiety and despair is that anxiety is the condition for the possibility of despair.[1] Also, the relationship between anxiety and sin after sin entails the relationship between anxiety and despair.[2] Just as the object of anxiety is altered depending on the type of sinfulness that one is in, so too the object of anxiety is altered in the various forms of despair. Since sin is despair before God, the relationship between anxiety and sin entails the relationship between anxiety and despair.

2. *Passages from* The Sickness Unto Death *on the Relationship*

When Kierkegaard wrote *The Sickness Unto Death*, he had already published *The Concept of Anxiety*. There are several explicit references to *The Concept of Anxiety* in *The Sickness Unto Death*. Therefore, when Anti-Climacus discusses the relationship between anxiety and despair in *The Sickness Unto Death*, this discussion is at least partly influenced by the analysis of anxiety in *The Concept of Anxiety*.

The term anxiety is only used eleven times in *The Sickness Unto Death*. As I will show in the next section, Kierkegaard was going to include a fairly lengthy section in which he explained the relationship between dizziness and despair. Though he does not explain what he means by dizziness, it is apparently a reference to anxiety. Vigilius had compared anxiety to dizziness and so it seems that the reference to dizziness is a reference to anxiety. However, Kierkegaard decided to remove most of this section from *The Sickness Unto Death*.[3] The passages in *The Sickness Unto Death* that are easiest to explain are those with explicit references to Vigilius. In explaining spiritlessness, Anti-Climacus refers to Vigilius's discussion of the anxiety of spiritlessness (*SUD*, 44). This reference to anxiety by Anti-Climacus is included solely in order to explain the meaning of spiritlessness.[4] Three pages later in *The Sickness Unto Death*, Anti-Climacus again explicitly refers to Vigilius and anxiety to borrow the distinction between paganism per se and paganism in Christendom (*SUD*, 47). Both of these references to Vigilius and *The Concept of Anxiety* are included by Anti-Climacus to explain some point other than the relationship between anxiety and despair.

There is another less explicit reference to Vigilius's concept of anxiety in *The Sickness Unto Death*. When Anti-

Climacus describes the sin of despairing over one's sin, he compares this to the anxiety of sin (*SUD*, 112). However, the point of this passage is not to explain the relationship between anxiety and despair, but to explain what Anti-Climacus means by selfishness.

There is one other reference to Vigilius's concept of anxiety, though it is much less clear than the others. In the opening passage, after the difficult explanation that the self is a relation that relates itself to itself and thereby relates itself to the power that established it, Anti-Climacus turns to the three kinds of despair. To explain what he means by despair, he says that it should not be confused with dizziness. Dizziness, writes Anti-Climacus, is something that happens to a person (*SUD*, 14). The reference to dizziness is apparently a reference to Vigilius's example that he uses to explain what he means by anxiety when he describes the feeling of looking out over the abyss. Vigilius wrote

> Anxiety may be compared with dizziness. He whose eye happens to look down into the yawning abyss becomes dizzy. But what is the reason for this? It is just as much in his own eye as in the abyss, for suppose he had not looked down. Hence anxiety is the dizziness of freedom that emerges when the spirit wants to posit the synthesis and freedom looks down into its own possibility, laying hold of finiteness to support itself (*CA*, 61).

Therefore, when Anti-Climacus refers to dizziness, he is apparently referring to anxiety.

Anti-Climacus's main point in discussing dizziness in *The Sickness Unto Death* is to show how despair is different from dizziness. The difference that Anti-Climacus points to is that dizziness happens to a person whereas despair is something brought about by the person (*SUD*, 14). His point here is that the individual is not responsible for dizziness, whereas the individual is responsible for despair. If one confuses despair with dizziness, one may not adequately recognize one's culpability for despair.

Two pages after this use of the concept of dizziness, Anti-Climacus refers to dizziness again (*SUD*, 16). Anti-Climacus repeats his point that despair differs from dizziness in that the individual is responsible for despair though not for dizziness. He then adds

> although qualitatively different, [despair] has much in common [with dizziness,] since dizziness corresponds, in the category of the psychical, to what despair is in the category of the spirit, and it lends itself to numerous analogies to despair (*SUD*, 16).[5]

When Anti-Climacus writes that the two are qualitatively different, he is reinforcing the idea that despair is the responsibility of the individual whereas dizziness is not. It is unclear if dizziness is to be understood as being identical to anxiety. Vigilius uses the experience of dizziness to explain the feeling of anxiety. Though the two feelings are similar, it is not clear that dizziness refers to one's attraction to and repulsion from future possibilities. Further, we saw in Chapter Three that anxiety is not a sickness.[6] However, the term dizziness does connote sickness, or at least is a state of "dis-ease." Further, dizziness seems to be used here to refer solely to an affect. Anti-Climacus does not make explicit reference here to the structural relation of the self to the future. Hence, when Anti-Climacus claims that dizziness is to the psychical as despair is to the spiritual, this may be taken as a claim about the affective similarity between the two. Both despair and dizziness are feelings that one has when faced with future possibilities. However, as structural conditions of the self, the two are qualitatively different, since despair is chosen whereas dizziness is not.

The only remaining references to anxiety in *The Sickness Unto Death* are passages where the term anxiety is not used in its technical sense. In the section where Anti-Climacus is seeking to encourage the reader to reflect upon one's own despair, he writes

> Just as a physician might say that there is very likely not
> one single living human being who is completely healthy,
> so anyone who really knows mankind might say that there
> is not one single living human being who does not de-
> spair a little, who does not secretly harbor an unrest, an
> inner strife, a disharmony, an *anxiety* about an unknown
> something or something he does not even dare to try to
> know, an *anxiety* about some possibility in existence or
> an *anxiety* about himself, so that, just as the physician
> speaks of going around with an illness in the body, he
> walks around with a sickness, carries around a sickness
> of the spirit that signals its presence at rare intervals in
> and through an *anxiety* he cannot explain (*SUD*, 16,
> emphasis mine).

It is curious that in this passage, Anti-Climacus seems to
equate anxiety and despair. However, given all that we
have previously seen, the technical meaning of anxiety
that Vigilius explained is not equivalent to the technical
meaning of despair explained by Anti-Climacus. There
are three explanations for this anomalous passage. First,
Anti-Climacus is here rhetorically trying to persuade the
reader to self-reflection to recognize one's own despair.[7]
In his zeal to bring about this end, he has used the term
anxiety to get the reader to recognize one's own wrongful use of freedom, i.e., despair. Second, anxiety is not
being used here in its developed technical sense. Anxiety
in this passage is equated with despair, inner strife and
disharmony. Anxiety is not being used here in Vigilius's
sense to mean the self's attraction to and repulsion from
future possibilities. Third, the kind of anxiety that Anti-
Climacus is suggesting that the reader might find is one
where the individual keeps himself unaware of the anxiety. But if one keeps oneself unaware of one's anxiety,
then one is willfully refusing to be oneself. Therefore,
though Anti-Climacus refers to anxiety, he is seeking to
cause the reader to recognize how one keeps oneself
unaware of one's anxiety and hence is willfully refusing
to be oneself. Hence, this passage should not be taken as

representing Kierkegaard's views on the relationship between anxiety and despair in their developed technical senses.

3. Passages from the Journals on the Relationship

We have seen that the relationship between anxiety and despair is not made explicit in either *The Concept of Anxiety* or *The Sickness Unto Death*. When we turn to the *Journals*, though there is no explicit discussion of the relationship between anxiety and despair, there are some extended passages on the relationship between dizziness and despair. These passages were written during the time of writing *The Sickness Unto Death*. Kierkegaard had intended to include them in the book, but later decided to delete them.

In the previous section, we saw that the term dizziness is used to connote anxiety. The link between dizziness and anxiety is based on a single passage in *The Concept of Anxiety* where Vigilius writes that "anxiety may be compared with dizziness" (*CA*, 61). Both in *The Sickness Unto Death* and in the *Journals*, it is not clear if Kierkegaard intends for the term dizziness to be identical with anxiety, particularly in the technical sense that is developed in *The Concept of Anxiety*. There is no clear explanation of the concept of dizziness in these passages from the *Journals*. Further, there seems to be at least several differences between anxiety and dizziness.[8] First, in ordinary language (both Danish and English), anxiety usually connotes an affective, psychological state while dizziness usually connotes a physical state. Second, dizziness is more associated with illness than is anxiety. As we saw in Chapter Three, Vigilius does not understand anxiety itself to be an illness; it is the last psychological state that precedes the wrongful use of freedom. Dizziness seems to differ from anxiety in that dizziness is a physical malady whereas anxiety is a psychological state that is not necessarily an illness. Therefore, since there are these differences between dizziness and anxiety, it is not clear that what Kierkegaard writes in his *Journals* about the relationship between dizziness and despair can be interpreted to be statements about the relationship between anxiety and despair.

There is another problem in interpreting his writings in the *Journals* on the relationship between dizziness and despair. It is not clear why Kierkegaard deleted these passages. With most authors, if a passage is deleted from the text, it usually signifies simply that the author thought the passage did not adequately express the point that was being made. However, with Kierkegaard and his indirect style, sometimes a passage is deleted because it expresses a point too explicitly. The *Journals* then are filled with a variety of types of passages. Some are first attempts at the expression of a particular point. Others are thoughts that Kierkegaard had recorded for possible future use. Some are passages that he probably considered too personal to include in his published work. Finally, some are deletions from texts that he went on to publish. The passages on the relationship between dizziness and despair seem simply to be deletions from a draft of the manuscript.

Kierkegaard explained some of his deletions from the text of *The Sickness Unto Death* when he wrote "It is best to remove the allusions to the dogma of hereditary sin which are found especially in chapter two (and anywhere else they are found.) It would take me too far out, or farther than is needed here or is useful" (*SKJP* 5, 6139). The references to hereditary sin would likely include the references to dizziness, since Vigilius had compared dizziness to anxiety in his "simple psychological deliberation on the dogmatic issue of hereditary sin."[9] Therefore, there is evidence that Kierkegaard was dissatisfied with his own writing on the relationship between dizziness and despair and hence decided to delete most of what he had written on the relationship from the manuscript. Consequently, since dizziness is not necessarily identical with anxiety and since Kierkegaard decided to delete this section from the book, it is most likely that what is written on the relationship between dizziness and despair in the *Journals* does not represent a fully developed explanation of Kierkegaard's view of the relationship between anxiety and despair.

The longest passage from the *Journals* on the relationship between dizziness and despair is titled "Despair is Like Being Dizzy or Dizziness, Yet Essentially (Qualitatively) Different" (*SKJP* 1, 749). Kierkegaard divides this section into five numbered parts. A later entry includes a sixth part. However, there are not six distinct points. Rather, there are essentially only two points made concerning the relationship between despair and dizziness. The clearest is the point of contrast. Despair is essentially or qualitatively different from dizziness since despair is the responsibility of the individual whereas dizziness is not. Kierkegaard expresses this difference in a number of ways. He writes "A person may be afflicted with dizziness, but never with despair" (*SKJP* 1, 749). In the same passage, he writes "the difference is that despair is related to spirit, to freedom, to responsibility."

Kierkegaard states several times in this entry that dizziness is similar to or may be compared with despair. At one point, he says the two are "pregnant with analogies" (*SKJP* 1, 749). However, he does not make explicit what the similarity is. He does state here in his *Journals* the ratio that he included in the text of *The Sickness Unto Death*: dizziness is to the psyche as despair is to the spirit (*SKJP* 1, 749). However, it is unclear what is meant by this comparison. It cannot mean that the simultaneous attraction to and repulsion from future possibilities is the same thing psychically as the misrelation of the self to itself is spiritually. Rather, the comparison is a comparison of the two considered as affects. Dizziness sometimes feels like despair. Both are negative, undesirable feelings. Still, Kierkegaard is never clear on showing how it is that both feelings are similar. Hence, this passage on the relationship between dizziness and despair yields two points: the feeling of despair is similar to the feeling of dizziness, but despair as a structure of one's being is essentially different since it is the responsibility of the individual.

There is another entry on the relationship between despair and dizziness that was to be included in *The Sickness Unto Death* that Kierkegaard deleted from the book. It was to follow the section just discussed and is titled "Despair Elucidated by Comparison with the Nevertheless Qualitatively Different or Vertigo."[10] This section is apparently abbreviated before the main point is developed. Kierkegaard begins by attempting to distinguish between physical and psychical dizziness. However, before he is able to explain the distinction, the entry is cut short. However, the title of this section makes the same point as was made in the previous section: though despair may feel like dizziness, it is qualitatively different.

The journal entries on the relationship between dizziness and despair make it clear that Kierkegaard holds that though there is a similarity between the feelings of despair and dizziness, despair differs inasmuch as it is the responsibility of the individual. However, Kierkegaard does not make clear the relationship between anxiety understood in the technical sense developed in *The Concept of Anxiety* and the technical meaning of despair that is set forth in *The Sickness Unto Death*. I turn now to that task. In the remaining sections, I will bring to light the relationship between Kierkegaard's developed concepts of anxiety and despair.

4. The Original Relationship Between Anxiety and Despair

In the preceding parts, I showed that Kierkegaard's pseudonyms use the terms anxiety and despair to refer not only to affects but more importantly to the structure of one's being that underlies the affect. Vigilius Haufniensis uses anxiety to denote the feeling of apprehensive eagerness, though more fundamentally he uses the term anxiety to refer to a relationship of both attraction and repulsion to a future possibility. In a similar way, Anti-Climacus uses the term despair to refer to the feeling that nothing matters, though more fundamentally he uses the term despair to refer to a misrelation in the self that is brought about by the self. In clarifying the concepts of anxiety and despair, both Vigilius and Anti-Climacus focus on the structure of human being that underlies each affect. Therefore, in seeking to make explicit the relationship between anxiety and despair, I will follow Kierkegaard's pseudonyms and focus on anxiety as the simultaneous attraction to and repulsion from the future and despair as a misrelation in the self that is brought about by the self.

I showed in chapter three that according to Vigilius, all human beings at all times are in anxiety. Since anxiety is one's ambiguous relationship to the future and since human beings are related to the future by being both attracted to and repulsed from possibility, anxiety is part of the structure of all human beings. One becomes conscious of one's anxiety, that is, of one's ambiguous relationship to the future, when faced with the moment of choice. However, the ambiguous relationship to the future that is the mark of human freedom precedes consciousness of it.

I showed in chapter five that, according to Anti-Climacus, human beings are not born in despair. Rather, despair is a condition brought about by oneself. Therefore, the original relationship between anxiety and despair in a human being is as follows. Anxiety precedes despair and is the condition for the possibility of despair. Because human beings are in anxiety, and because humans are both attracted to and repulsed from the future, humans are free. If a human were strictly attracted to certain possibilities and repulsed from other possibilities, then there would be no freedom of choice. Despair is the wrongful use of this freedom of choice. Hence, anxiety precedes the first instance of despair both logically and temporally. Logically, freedom of choice is the condition for the possibility of the wrongful use of freedom. Since anxiety, the simultaneous attraction to and repulsion from future possibilities is what makes human beings free and since despair is the wrongful use of freedom, anxiety is the condition for the possibility of despair. Likewise, anxiety precedes despair temporally. This is made clear from the earlier claim that anxiety is the state of all human beings whereas despair is a later state brought about by the self.

When Vigilius describes the anxiety of Adam prior to the first sin, he is describing the original relationship between anxiety and despair.[11] Sin, as we have seen, is despair before God.[12] Vigilius's description of Adam's anxiety is also a description of an experience repeated by every human being who wrongfully uses freedom. Just as for Adam, in Vigilius's description, anxiety preceded the first sin, so too for everyone who wrongfully uses freedom, anxiety precedes despair and is the condition for the possibility of despair.[13]

5. Anxiety and Despair as Each Relates to Spiritlessness

The theme of spiritlessness is taken up in both *The Concept of Anxiety* and *The Sickness Unto Death*.

Spiritlessness is the unawareness that the task of human life is to be oneself. In particular, spiritlessness is the vincible ignorance that one is to be a self. The unconsciousness of spiritlessness is one for which the human being is culpable. In this way, spiritlessness is an unconsciousness of one's task to be a self that is willfully brought about by the person.

Spiritlessness is not a misrelation in the self in the same sense that either the despair of weakness or the despair of defiance is a misrelation in the self. Rather, spiritlessness is a form of ignorance that makes it impossible for a human being to recognize that one is a self. When there is no recognition that there is a self, there is not a willed misrelation in the self. Hence, Anti-Climacus says that spiritlessness is not properly a form of despair (*SUD*, 13-4). Yet, since this unawareness of one's task to be a self is brought about willfully by oneself, through cunning and self-deception, so much so that one does not recognize it as self-deception, spiritlessness is closely related to despair. While spiritlessness is not a willed misrelation in the self, it is a willed ignorance of one's task to be a self. Hence, it has the same result as despair, namely, the human being fails to be a self. If anything, it is worse than despair, for spiritlessness is not only failure to be a self, it does not recognize its own failure.

Both Vigilius and Anti-Climacus distinguish between the spiritlessness of paganism and spiritlessness in Christendom (*CA*, 93-6; *SUD*, 45-7). Anti-Climacus makes the distinction between the two by explicitly referring to the same distinction already made by Vigilius in *The Concept of Anxiety* (*SUD*, 47). Paganism lacks the explicit revelation given in Christianity that one is a self before God. Anti-Climacus brings up the example of suicide to show that pagan cultures did not have an adequate notion of the self. Those pagan thinkers, in particular the Stoics, who held that suicide was permissible, did so because they did not recognize that a human being is a self before God and that to commit suicide is to mutiny against God. Still, some non-Christian thinkers were able to arrive at this insight without Christian revelation, for example, Socrates, as presented by Plato in the *Phaedo* at 62c, held that suicide was a violation of the desires of God. Still, Socrates was not adequately aware of one's total dependence on God or of one's need for redemption. Therefore, spiritlessness in paganism is the unawareness that a human being is a self that is completely dependent on God. The non-Christian may have insight in this direction. Thus, spiritlessness in paganism is only culpable to the degree one has willfully ignored one's task to be a self and to the degree this task can be known without divine revelation.

In Christendom, spiritlessness is still the unawareness of one's task to be a self, though it is more culpable. It is more culpable than spiritlessness in paganism because those in Christendom have access to the Christian revelation that makes it clear that one is a self before God and dependent on God. Therefore, spiritlessness in Christendom "lacks spirit in a departure from spirit or in a falling away and therefore is spiritlessness in the strictest sense" (*SUD*, 47).

The anxiety of spiritlessness is a particular kind of anxiety. There is a logical connection between spiritlessness and the anxiety of spiritlessness, for only spiritlessness undergoes the anxiety of spiritlessness. The anxiety of spiritlessness is the anxiety of those who have willfully ignored the task to be a self through self-deception. This form of anxiety is not felt, for the person ignores the relationship to the future. There is no strong feeling of apprehension or of eagerness. Still, the anxiety remains, though the person is unaware of it. The spiritless person still has a relationship to the future of simultaneous attraction and repulsion. Ignoring this does not abolish it.

Therefore, in spiritlessness, anxiety and despair have a new relationship. The person is one step away from despair through ignorance. Before one can despair, that is, willfully bring about a misrelation in the self, there must be some recognition that one is a self. Spiritlessness ignores anxiety, for in ignoring that one's task is to be a self, one also ignores one's free relationship to the future. However, though the spiritless person is unaware of it, anxiety remains since there is still a relationship to the future of attraction and repulsion.

6. Anxiety and Despair as Each Relates to Inclosing Reserve

In the preceding chapters, I showed that both Vigilius and Anti-Climacus take up the topic of inclosing reserve.[14] Inclosing reserve differs from spiritlessness in its consciousness of the self. In spiritlessness, the self wills to keep itself unaware that its task is to become itself. In inclosing reserve, there is an awareness of the self. However, instead of choosing to be oneself, one closes in upon oneself and becomes shut up within oneself. In this section I will examine the relation between anxiety and despair as each relates to inclosing reserve.

In *The Concept of Anxiety*, Vigilius claims that the anxiety of the good is inclosing reserve. However, this point is not adequately expressed. The anxiety of the good is the ambiguous relation to the possibility of redemption. This relation to the good of both attraction and repulsion that is the anxiety is not itself willed. The individual always retains a relation to the good (*CA*, 123). Within this relation to the good where the individual is both attracted to and repulsed from the possibility of redemption, the individual willfully turns away from the good. This willfully turning away from the good is inclosing reserve. Vigilius's point is that even having willfully turned away from the good and having closed in upon oneself, one continues to be partially attracted to the good. This attraction to the good is ignored; it only becomes manifest when one is explicitly in this presence of the good. Hence, Vigilius takes the outbursts of the demonic in the presence of Christ to be examples of the anxiety of the good exhibiting itself.

The willing to close oneself in upon oneself is a misrelation to oneself and hence is a kind of despair. In *The Sickness Unto Death*, Anti-Climacus describes two types of inclosing reserve. In the first type, there is some recognition of one's task to be a self. However, instead of taking up the task of being a self, one closes in upon oneself to hide from one's task. The externalities of one's life continue, but deep within oneself, one becomes enclosed. In a paradox of self-evasion, one closes oneself off from oneself. This form of inclosing reserve is a kind of the despair of weakness, since it is an unwillingness to be oneself. The second type of inclosing reserve that Anti-Climacus describes is a turning in upon oneself in defiance. Here, there is the recognition both that one is a self and that one is in relation to God. However, in pride one turns away from God and in upon oneself, closing oneself off from the possibility of redemption. This form of inclosing reserve, which Anti-Climacus describes in the section on the despair of defiance, is the same form of inclosing reserve that Vigilius refers to in *The Concept of Anxiety*. (*SUD*, 72-3; *CA*, 123ff). Since Vigilius's goal is to describe and explain anxiety and since inclosing reserve is not itself anxiety, he does not give an account of inclosing reserve. Rather, he describes inclosing reserve only so far as is necessary to make clear his description and explanation of the anxiety of the good. This inclosing reserve where one defiantly turns in upon oneself and away from the good (God) is a kind of despair since it entails a misrelation in the self. The misrelation in the self is a misrelation to God; since the self is dependent on God, when in inclosing reserve one turns in upon oneself and refuses to recognize one's dependence on God, one is thereby misrelated to oneself. Therefore, inclosing reserve is a form of despair.

There is a conceptual connection between the anxiety of the good that Vigilius describes and the inclosing reserve described by Anti-Climacus. Vigilius describes the relation to the good of an individual who has defiantly turned inward. The shutting up within oneself is despair; it is a misrelation to oneself since it is a willing to be a self other than what one is. The relation to the good of one who has defiantly turned inward is one of both attraction and repulsion. Vigilius's point is that even though this person defiantly denies any attraction to the good, this attraction remains. This attraction mixed with repulsion is the anxiety. The willful turning of oneself in upon oneself is a form of despair. Therefore, the person whom Vigilius describes in the section on the anxiety of the good is both in anxiety and in despair. The anxiety of this person is the anxiety of the good that is a simultaneous attraction to and repulsion from the possibility of redemption offered by God. The despair of this person is the refusal to be oneself. It is the defiant willing to be a self independent of God and since the self is dependent on God, hence is a willing to be a self that one is not. Therefore, though these two structures are conceptually connected, there is a clear distinction between the anxiety of the good and inclosing reserve.[15]

7. The Role of Anxiety in Overcoming Despair

Kierkegaard holds that the only way that sin, that is, despair before God, may be overcome is by faith in the salvific act of Christ. However, anxiety has an important role to play and is a necessary condition for the possibility of overcoming despair.

The individual in despair has wrongfully used freedom. Before God, the person is in sin. There are four responses to this state of sin that the individual may take. First, this person may attempt to overcome despair by "doing the best one can." The individual may turn in upon oneself and defiantly attempt to be oneself on one's own. However, this attempt to redeem oneself is always a failed attempt, for it never changes one's past and present despair. Therefore, the attempt to overcome despair on one's own is simply another form of despair. It is a new refusal to be oneself. Anti-Climacus refers to this as this sin of despairing over one's sin (*SUD*, 109-113). A second response is to despair of the forgiveness of sins. The individual may have a clear consciousness of Christ and Christ's claim that he offers forgiveness. However, the person is offended by this claim and despairs of the forgiveness of sins (*SUD*, 113-125). A third response that the person in despair before God may have is positively to reject Christianity as untruth. (*SUD*, 125ff). This is a more intensified response than the previous one. Here, the individual does not only despair of the possibility of forgiveness, the person willfully and defiantly rejects Christianity as an untruth. A fourth response is, of course, to accept Christ's claim that he is the God-man and that through him comes the forgiveness of sins. I will turn to a more complete analysis of this last response.

In order that an individual who is in despair before God may turn to God and accept Christ's claim that he is the God-man and through him sins are forgiven, anxiety must necessarily be present. The individual in despair has willfully misused freedom by choosing to be a self that one is not. In doing so, the self becomes closed up within itself. In order to break out of this despair, one needs to have some relation to the future. The individual's relationship to the future is anxiety. In anxiety, one is both attracted to and repulsed from the possibility of redemption. However, the acceptance of God's grace in Christ's salvific act is a choice that, if made, must be made in anxiety. The individual is both attracted to and repulsed from the future possibility of redemption. The choice to accept God's grace and the forgiveness of sins is a choice made in anxiety. Through faith, which is the acceptance of the forgiveness of Christ, despair is overcome. Therefore, anxiety is a necessary condition for the possibility of overcoming despair, according to Kierkegaard.

Finally, despair is overcome through the forgiveness of sins. Christ's salvific act rights the misrelation in the self through forgiveness. Salvation does not entail the restructuring of the self such that despair is never again a possibility. Rather, as I have shown, according to Kierkegaard, anxiety is essential to human being. After salvation, the individual continues to be in anxiety. There is still a simultaneous attraction to and repulsion from the possibility of future sins. From this, it would follow that the individual may fall into despair again after redemption. Since anxiety is part of the structure of human being, despair is always a future possibility. Redemption, even the redemptive act of Christ, does not negate anxiety from human existence. Hence, despair is overcome by redemption only in the sense that there is a forgiveness of sins, not in the sense that the possibility of ever sinning again is negated.

With this understanding of the relationship between anxiety and despair in Kierkegaard's thought, we turn now to the more fully examine what Kierkegaard's writings can teach us about freedom and its misuses.

CHAPTER 7

Freedom and Its Misuses

1. Four Senses of "Freedom" in Kierkegaard

Implied in Kierkegaard's analysis of anxiety and despair, the term freedom[1] is used in four distinct senses.[2] After tracing those four, I will later show how they fit together.

A. Freedom from a Force Outside of One's Control

Kierkegaard occasionally used the term freedom to mean exemption from a force outside of one's control, though this sense is not developed in detail in his writing, nor is it primary in Kierkegaard's thought. In Danish, *frihed* (freedom) is followed by the preposition *for* (from) when used in this sense, as in the English phrase "freedom from," for example, freedom from pain, freedom from undue taxation, freedom from worry. In liberal democracies, appeals to this kind of freedom are made when there are calls for freedom from the constraints of an oppressive government. Therefore, related to the freedom from a force outside of one's control are the civic and political liberties associated with modern liberal democracy: freedom of the press, freedom of speech, freedom of religion.

Each of these refer to the state of being exempt from a force outside of one's control.

In his *Journals,* Kierkegaard writes explicitly of this kind of freedom, of freedom of belief and freedom of conscience, though he criticizes people of his age for thinking that freedom of conscience comes from alleviating the constraints of the state (*SKJP* 2, 1264). In another entry, Kierkegaard again chides his era, writing "People almost never make use of the freedoms they have, for example, freedom of thought; by way of compensation they demand freedom of expression instead" (*SKJP* 2, 1236). The term freedom is used in the same sense in *Either/Or Vol. 1,* when the seducer describes how he must not force Cordelia, stating "she must be free," that is, in order to achieve the desired state of pleasure that drives the seducer, Cordelia must come to him without constraints, free from external control, for only then does he find enjoyment. In each of these instances, freedom means exemption from outside constraints.

In British and American political philosophy, this kind of freedom has been central. Thomas Jefferson's appeal to a self-evident right to liberty refers to the freedom from external control. Likewise, Locke wrote of the individual's freedom from outside constraints, especially an oppressive government. Individual liberty, as a political right, can be seen as grounded in the claim that a human being ought to be free from external control.[3]

This aspect of freedom can be construed in either a descriptive or a normative sense. A slave who becomes unbound may be described as acquiring freedom, just as Kierkegaard's father, who was tied to the land as a feudal serf in childhood, received his freedom. On the other hand, freedom from external constraint can be understood as a moral and political right, more than a description, but a prescription of how human beings ought to be treated. Jefferson's appeal to liberty in "The Declaration of Independence," as well as Locke's in his *Second Treatise on Government*, refer to normative claims about freedom from external control. Likewise, freedom of speech, freedom of religion, freedom of the press, and the wide range of political freedoms associated with liberal democracy all use the term freedom to mean freedom from external constraint. While Kierkegaard did not emphasize this aspect of freedom, he did occasionally use the term freedom to mean freedom from outside control.

However, part of the key to Kierkegaard's analysis of freedom is that an overemphasis on "freedom from" ends up making real freedom impossible.[4] Freedom from external constraint leaves one bound up within oneself. Once one has overcome the tyranny of external control, we become tyrants to ourselves.[5] When individual freedom faces external constraint, it has a clear battle to fight. But, as Robert Bellah has explained with reference to American individualism, when there are no external constraints, this kind of freedom offers no guidance about how to live well.[6] The result is a feeling of being alone, lost in a world of possibility. Having freed itself from others, the self ends up feeling alone, absorbed in itself until the self begins to run away from itself. In this way, when freedom from external constraint is crowned, it becomes a ravenous ruler, a power without guidance.

Of course some defenders of this kind of freedom will say that the freedom from external constraints has some clearly specifiable limits. An oppressive government should not control its citizens, but neither should its citizens seek to control one another. My freedom ends where your freedom begins. This does little to say what I should do with my freedom, but it does point to an important insight: freedom is fundamentally relational. Kierkegaard develops this idea, but in a direction slightly different from the sociological perspective that tries to make freedom communal.[7] As we will see below, Kierkegaard maintains that freedom is relational, but not simply in the sense of living in right relation to others, but also in right relation to oneself and to God.

The freedom from external constraint, though it has been canonized in our culture, is not the fundamental meaning of freedom, and surely not so for Kierkegaard.[8] Freedom from external constraint gets its importance because of freedom of choice. Locke and Jefferson knew this in their appeals to natural law and natural rights. Human beings are endowed with freedom of choice, so for a government to deny its citizens freedom is to treat them as less than human. Therefore, an account of freedom from external constraint should be followed by an account of free choice.

B. Freedom of Choice

One of the important meanings of freedom in Kierkegaard's writing is freedom of choice. Kierkegaard is well aware of the freedom/determinism debate that has marked modern philosophy, and he solves the problem in a novel way. Traditionally, the problem of free choice centers around the attempt to maintain individual moral responsibility while accounting for scientific causal determinism. An overemphasis on freedom seems to imply arbitrariness and the demise of science. An overemphasis on causal determinism seems to imply the downfall of personal responsibility. The classic solution to the problem in modernity is Kant's. He solved the problem by dividing the world in two. The world of experience is scientifically determined according to the laws of cause and effect. But at the noumenal level, the self is free. The effect is that it is possible to have a causally determined world where individuals have freedom of choice so that moral responsibility is saved, but only by separating the self from the world of lived experience.

Kierkegaard's approach to the problem of freedom of choice begins by examining the self as a being in the world, a self with passions and desires, with flesh and facticity, and yet a self with language, memory and imagination, a self in time, but a self that has an aspect of eternity. The affective life, and in particular the experience of anxiety, provides insight into human freedom. Anxiety, as we have seen, is more than a simple brooding disposition of a melancholy Dane. It is the simultaneous attraction to and repulsion from a future possibility that is not yet. This anxiety is more than a feeling. It is the mark of human freedom. If one's relation to a future possibility was simply attraction, as an ant's to a pheromone, then behavior would be causally determined, because the attractive object would determine the behavior. Or if one's relation to a future possibility was solely repulsion, as a gorilla that flees when water buffalo come near, then behavior would be causally determined, for the repulsive object would determine the behavior. But the human self is related to future possibilities in anxiety, that is, by both attraction and repulsion. Humans turn away from the desirable, even while approaching it. When humans flee from water buffalo, or anything repulsive, there is a secret urge to look back, to get closer. This anxiety, the simultaneous attraction and repulsion, is the mark of being able. We approach, though we can turn away. We flee, though we needn't. Anxiety is the mark of the possibility of possibility, which is the actuality of free choice.

This freedom of choice is not a freedom of arbitrariness. Some want to insist that choice is free only if it is arbitrary and entirely unpredictable. But this is based on a confusion in method, a confusion between a self-reflective method and the method of empirical psychology. Just because the action of someone else can be observed and then predicted does not mean it is causally determined. It may mean that the person being observed is self-disciplined and self-controlled. Similarly, if a person's behavior is entirely unpredictable, this is not necessarily a sign that the behavior is free. Instead, a person whose actions are unpredictable may be neurotic or psychotic, the victim of some controlling desire or warped sensibility that is as yet not well understood by the observer. The unpredictable behavior of another is not good evidence for free choice. Instead, the best access to freedom of choice is phenomenological self-reflection. A free choice is one made in anxiety, that is, where one is both attracted and repulsed to the future possibility. Though the attraction may be great and the repulsion slight, or the reverse, self-reflection can show that a choice was made, and that the individual is in some way responsible for that choice.

In this sense, the opposite of freedom of choice is the causal determinism of not being able to do anything other than what one does. There is no freedom of choice in a rock that falls, a piece of metal that is attracted to a magnet, an animal that approaches or flees. Neither is there freedom of choice in an ordinary sneeze. So when freedom is understood in the sense of free choice, of being able, its opposite is the compulsion of necessity.

This account of free choice does not abolish psychology as a science. It may seem that if this view of free choice is correct, then psychology cannot be a science. After all, a science cannot gain knowledge about randomness. But even given this view of free choice, psychology continues to be a science in two specific ways. First, psychology can describe the state of individuals before choice. This is a descriptive task, and one suitable for psychology. Second, psychology can seek to understand conditioning factors. After all, the free choice that is evidenced through an analysis of anxiety does not deny the role of conditioning factors in the environment. It only denies that the environment is a determining factor. A particular environment may condition an individual so that certain future possibilities are more attractive and less repulsive, while an altered environment may make similar future possibilities seem less attractive and more repulsive. Psychology can continue to study conditioning factors as a worthwhile scientific endeavor. However, to confuse conditioning factors with determining factors is to falsify psychology, to misunderstand the human self, and to deny the freedom of choice made evident by a phenomenological self-analysis of anxiety.

In this way, one of the meanings of freedom for Kierkegaard is being able, the possibility of possibility made evident by anxiety, which is to say that on Kierkegaard's view, humans have free choice.

C. The Self is Freedom

Kierkegaard uses the term freedom in a different sense when he has Anti-Climacus write "the self is freedom" (*SUD*, 29). This is the primary way that the term freedom is used in *The Sickness Unto Death*, though it is also used this way in *The Concept of Anxiety*. For example, in reference to a young man, Vigilius writes "In turning inward, he discovers freedom" (*CA*, 108). And even more explicitly, we see the two distinct uses of the term·freedom when Vigilius writes of an individual that has the "freedom to know of himself that he is freedom." (*CA*, 108). In the first sense, freedom is akin to freedom of choice, for it is the ability to be aware of himself; this is the freedom of being able. In the second sense, freedom is not choice but the self.

In this sense, freedom means self-actualization. This sense of freedom denotes being oneself, that is, living in right relation to oneself, (and to others), and ultimately also to God. This is made clearer when Vigilius goes on to contrast this sense of freedom with its opposite: guilt (*CA*, 108). Freedom in the sense of self-actualization occurs when the self becomes itself by choosing to be itself.

When the self misuses its freedom of choice, choosing to be something other than itself, the result is guilt.

Guilt has both a subjective and an objective element. Subjectively, guilt shows itself in the feeling of shame. Objectively, guilt is the misrelation in the self brought about by the wrongful use of the freedom of choice. So freedom in this sense is being oneself, while the opposite of the freedom of self-actualization is guilt.

Vigilius expresses this aspect of freedom when he writes "The good is freedom" (*CA*, 111). Considered merely from the perspective of free choice, where freedom means "being able" there is a temptation to say that before one chooses, one is faced with a choice between good and evil. But, as Judge William explained in *Either/Or Vol. 2*, before one can choose between good and evil, one must choose choice (*E/O* II, L227-30, H222-26).

Kierkegaard's teaching on this point has been complicated by Alasdair MacIntyre's serious misinterpretation, not only in *After Virtue* (1984, 40-44), but also in his entry on Kierkegaard in *The Encyclopedia of Philosophy*.[9] MacIntyre tries to paint Kierkegaard as the villain in the decay of morality in the modern world, or at least as a symptom of irrational relativism in contemporary ethics. He does this by twisting Kierkegaard's notion of choice and his teaching on freedom. In particular, MacIntyre fails to distinguish between the freedom of choice and the freedom of self-actualization. MacIntyre's fault on this point is even more serious than it might first seem, for though he states in *After Virtue* that his interpretation is out of line with the best Kierkegaard commentators, and it is evident enough that he doesn't really have any textual evidence to support the caricature that he presents to extend his own attack on modernity, his entry in the *Encyclopedia* (where fairness is most expected) gives no hint that his is a twisted interpretation out of line with the best scholars in the field.

By failing to distinguish between freedom of choice and freedom of self-actualization, MacIntyre turns Kierkegaard into an inconsistent irrationalist. The irony in this is not only that MacIntyre viciously twists Kierkegaard to further his own argument about virtue, but that he ends up missing Kierkegaard's emphasis on virtue and the importance of forming one's character. Kierkegaard's teaching on choice, as expressed both by Judge William and by Vigilius, is this. Before one chooses, one has the possibility to choose. In that sense, one has freedom of choice. But as one becomes aware of the possibility of choice, one is also becoming aware that to be oneself means to be a self that is capable of choosing. With this awareness, not choosing, not taking responsibility for one's choices, is precisely the choice not to be oneself. For choice to be actual, it need not entail two equally desirable alternatives. The choice not to be oneself is a choice, a bad one, but still a choice. Further, it is a choice made all too often.

Yet there is another aspect of freedom besides free choice, namely the freedom of self-actualization. This is the freedom of being oneself. This kind of self-actualization is good, for a reason similar to why a mature oak tree is good while an acorn has that same goodness only in potentiality. Actualization is good. But the oak tree becomes actualized through environmental factors, while the self, because of consciousness and freedom, becomes actualized through choice.

Before one chooses between good and evil, one responds to one's environment according to pleasure and displeasure, that is, according to immediate gratification, self-interest, or social expectations. For one to begin making choices, one must first begin to take responsibility for one's choices. Choice entails the recognition of personal responsibility. Otherwise, what appears to be a choice between good and evil will in fact be a conditioned response based on pleasure, self-interest, immediate gratification or social expectations. So in order for there to be a choice between good and evil, there must first be a choice that one will take responsibility for one's choices. Having made that choice, one is then being oneself, at least to a greater degree than before, for to be a self means to be a self-conscious agent with free choice. Thus, to choose choice is to choose to be oneself. The choice between good and evil then becomes the choice either to be oneself or not.

Since the self is a self among other selves, this move into choice carries with it all of the moral obligations and duties that go with Kant's categorical imperative. Judge William uses an existential path through despairing of immediate gratification to arrive at Kant's ethic of duty. He refers to universalizability as a criterion for moral decision making, and implicitly appeals to respect for oneself and for others (*E/O* II, L333ff, H328ff). Just as the motive for Kant's ethic is self-referential, that is, rational creatures should treat rational creatures as rational creatures because it is rational, so the Judge's ethic states that one should be oneself, a self-conscious agent with free choice, because that is who one is. Goodness then means being oneself. The criterion for goodness is the same for Kierkegaard as it is for the old natural law philosophy: be yourself. The difference is that Kierkegaard has a different understanding of the self. Instead of understanding the human being through the metaphysics of hylomorphism, or as an embodied soul, he understands the human self to be a relation between soul and body, a relation that relates itself to itself, that is, a spirit, a relation that can choose to become a self-conscious agent with free choice.

In this sense, the self is freedom. Freedom understood in the sense of self-actualization is more akin to harmony than it is to decision making ability. If human beings always chose to be themselves, never deceived themselves, never treated themselves or others as if they were less than they are, never treated themselves or others as if there were more than they are, never tried to escape from themselves, never tried to pretend that they were God, then each free choice would result in the freedom of self-actualization. But as it is, free choice gets misused. As a consequence, being able to choose to be something other than oneself results in the opposite of self-actualization, in self-destruction. When an organism without free choice actualizes a potency, it matures, becoming more itself. But when an organism with free choice, a self, actualizes free choice, the self often chooses to be something other than itself, so that what began as self-actualization becomes a kind of spiritual self-destruction. Therefore, though the self is freedom, both in the sense that it has free choice and in the sense that its actualization is freedom, the concrete situation is that human selves have misused freedom. To misuse freedom solely with regard to oneself and others is to be guilty and immoral; to do so before God is sin.

Having misused our freedom, it remains true that the self is freedom in the sense that the actualization of the self is freedom, but the self has castrated itself, as it were, entangled itself in its own misuse of freedom, so that each new attempt to actualize itself is a failure. The self fails to be itself either by running away from itself or by defiantly claiming to be more than itself. And since the self is temporal and has a history, even those attempts at self-actualization that are successful for a moment cannot change one's past failures. And any current success at self-actualization that fails to rectify past failure is itself a failure, either because it does not rectify past failures or because it claims that past failures are past, and hence no longer a part of the self. But since the self is temporal, this is merely one more way of not being oneself. Consequently, the self that is freedom is left entangled, aware of its own shortcomings and unable to overcome them, in short, enslaved in sin.

D. Christ is our Freedom

Without the Christian revelation, it is possible to understand that the task of human life is to be a self, and that to be a self means to be a synthesis between the physical and the psychical, a relation that relates itself to itself, even a relation that is in relation to God. Further, it is possible to realize that though one has the task of selfhood, one is constantly falling short of the ideal. So without the Christian revelation, the problem of human life may be construed as the problem of overcoming moral shortcomings.

There are two likely solutions to the problem. First, one may resolve to try harder. After all, the problem now is not that one is totally ignorant of what to strive for, but that in striving, one falls short. This difficulty seems to be a problem in the self, so the solution should be found in the self. Work at it; try harder. Unfortunately, this ends up straining the self, seeming at times to be almost humanly impossible. So there is a second solution: lower the standard. It may have seemed that the task of life was to be a self, but repeatedly one notices that one is falling short of this task. Freud's recommendation to solve this problem was clear: for therapeutic purposes we are obliged to lower the demands of ethical obligation (1961, 101). The self can not bear to live up to the demands of ideality, so it should compromise by lowering the standards. This solution cushions one aspect of the self, but it disregards the validity of the moral demands of ideality.

A different diagnosis and cure is offered with the Christian revelation. In the person of Christ there is a different hope, a hope that is either freeing or offensive. It is the offer of redemption, the offer of the forgiveness of sins. Christ is our freedom in the sense that His redemptive grace offers the forgiveness of sins, such that the misuse of freedom is abolished. Through grace the self is brought into right relation with itself, others and God. Christ is our freedom in the sense that He restores the self to right relation, making the freedom of self-actualization possible by divine grace.

This teaching goes beyond human reason. The correct existential response is one of earnestness: it is either offensive or freeing. But if Christ is our freedom, then He frees us from our sins, thus making possible the freedom of self-actualization.

In this sense, the freedom of Christ is like the first kind of freedom, for Christ liberates the self from a force outside of its own control, that is, from its own sinfulness. Christ's freedom is a kind of freedom from, a freedom from sin.

2. Freedom and Individualism

Kierkegaard's teachings on anxiety and despair are sometimes grossly misinterpreted such that his stress on individualism is wedded with his discussion of anxiety and despair so that he is thought to espouse a lonely individualism. While I think that this view is fundamentally wrongheaded, it points to an ambiguity in the meaning of individualism in Kierkegaard.

On the one hand, Kierkegaard is a critic of egoism. The aesthetic life, where one merely responds to the environment according to self-interest, is repeatedly presented by Kierkegaard to be a life unbefitting true human selfhood. So if modern individualism means self-interest, doing whatever you want, living for the moment, answering to no one else, then Kierkegaard is a critic of the individualist turn in modern liberalism.

On the other hand, Kierkegaard does not criticize liberal individualism by contrasting it with a predominantly communal approach. He does not want to replace egoism with a worship of the group. Rather, the crowd is repeatedly criticized, for in the crowd one loses one's individuality. Kierkegaard criticized modern liberalism for reducing individuals into egoists so that they can each act independently, and then throwing them into a crowd where they all forfeit their independence while no one takes responsibility.

Kierkegaard's credo, the primary purpose in his writing, is "become yourself," and that means acting as an individual. The urge for his reader to become a Christian in Christendom, the driving motive in his authorship, points to a different kind of individualism. Instead of the individualism of self-interest, Kierkegaard urges the self-actualization where one lives in right relation to oneself, to others and to God. And in this self-actualization, just as Abraham's devotion to God was greater than to his own son, the relation to God is greater than the relation to others.

Kierkegaard never developed his teaching on this point clearly. He evidently had a difficult time with his relation to others, as he ended up living a relatively solitary life as an adult. In places, his writing stresses the individualism where one is a self alone before God. In fact, at times Kierkegaard seems to view others as a necessary evil to selves that can not bear to be alone with God.[10] In his journals, he writes "when the ideality of the God-relationship has become too strong for an individual . . ., he must now have another person to discuss it with. For this we see that sociality is not the highest, but is really a concession to human weakness" (*SKJP* 2, 1377). So on this view, individualism means being yourself, alone before God, and the relation to other selves is unimportant. Religious inwardness seems to be presented as all important, while concrete moral action is derided. The old Lutheran emphasis on faith without works seems to end up with a self like Kant's noumena, divorced from the concrete world of lived action.

Yet Kierkegaard is a Lutheran who is moved by James's Epistle, the letter that made Luther shake, with its emphasis on works and action. In his *Works of Love*, as well as in many other places, Kierkegaard gives great importance to the self's relation to other selves.[11] Love of neighbor is presented as a central human duty. To be oneself, to be an individual, means being a self in relation to other selves. There is evidence that Kierkegaard was trying to work out more fully the relation of the self to other selves. We have seen his account of the self as a relation that relates itself to itself, but there is a journal entry where Kierkegaard uses similar language to account for the self's relation to other selves. Using three different formulas, he describes the relation to other selves at (1) the aesthetic, (2) the ethical and (3) the religious levels.

> (1) the individuals who relate to each other in the relation are individually inferior to the relation. . . .
> (2) the individuals who relate to each other in the relation are individually equal in relation to the relation. . . .
> (3) the individuals who relate themselves to each other in the relation are individually superior to the relation (*SKJP* 4, 4110).

At the aesthetic level, the self has not yet become itself, and so the self does not take responsibility for the relation to others. At the ethical level, each self takes responsibility for oneself as well as for one's relation to others. At the religious level, the relation to other selves is teleologically suspended in the relation to God, though this does not obliterate the relation to others or the duties of moral action. The entry makes this clear when it goes on to explain that at the religious level, "the individual is primarily related to God and then to the community, but this primary relation is the highest, yet he does not neglect the second" (*SKJP* 4, 4110). It appears that this formula, though still perhaps unclear, means that in order to become oneself, which is ultimately to live in right relation to God, one must live in right relation to others. The religious life does not obliterate ethics and social obligation. Instead, when one's duty to God is made primary, one gets back one's duty to others, so that morality and the social life is elevated and sanctified, yet it is not idolized. On that interpretation, it is easier to understand the important place of the moral community in the religious life. Thus, Kierkegaard writes in his journals "When the state acquires its proper significance, to be exiled will become—as it was with the Greeks - the most severe punishment" (*SKJP* 4, 4073). Hence, to be an individual means to take responsibility for oneself by living in right relation to others, recognizing that if one cannot live in right relation to others, one cannot be oneself, and for one who has sinned, it is only possible to live up to the moral demands of ideality through Christ's redemptive grace. Thus, true individualism entails living in right relation to other selves in community, and yet true individualism does not idolize the community.

Nonetheless, Kierkegaard could have been clearer in explaining the self's relation to other selves. In particular, he could more fully show the relationship between anxiety and language, and between consciousness of the other as a self and self-consciousness. Further, he could have done more to give a phenomenological description of possible misrelations between the self and other selves. So while I do not think that Kierkegaard has fundamentally misconstrued the self's relation to others, he has misconstrued it in places, and in general he has not made his position as clear as he might have. Still, Kierkegaard's individualism is a long way from egoism, and is fundamentally an individualism that stresses responsibility, specifically responsibility for living in right relation to oneself, to others and to God.

3. The Misuses of Freedom

As we have seen in chapter five, *The Sickness Unto Death* offers an account of despair, that is, of the misuse of freedom. In *The Sickness Unto Death*, when freedom is mentioned, it refers to the freedom of self-actualization. But the misuse of freedom can be more fully analyzed using the distinctions between the four aspects of freedom outlined above.

When freedom is taken to mean freedom from a force outside of one's control, especially when this is construed as freedom from the government, the development of the self tends to get stuck at the level of self-interest. The appeal to freedom from outside force, though perhaps grounded in moral justice, often strikes home at the level of self-interested pleasure. Freedom becomes selfishness. I can do whatever I want. It is a free country. Consequently, the self shrinks in upon itself. Instead of feeling free, the self ends up feeling isolated and alone. Freedom from tyranny becomes isolation from others.

The situation is similar when freedom is taken to mean freedom of choice. Since freedom of choice can offer no criterion for choice, the self is faced with overwhelming possibility. Hence the self either shrinks away from choice, escaping freedom by identifying itself with something that it is not, or submitting itself to another as to an idol, or losing itself in the crowd. Or the self chooses, and chooses consciously, but chooses to be more than it is, chooses to be the ground of itself, something that it is not. With no ground but free choice, an ethics of freedom becomes an ethics of defiance. The self stands up boldly, shouting "I have chosen, I, myself. You can not choose for me." When a self does this to a tyrannical leader, we recognize that self as heroic and brave, but when the dictator is gone, then this self, so identifying freedom with free choice, defiantly shouts at everyone, at existence, at God. "I am my own person. I will carve my name in my chest with a razor blade. I will spurn the standards of society. I will laugh at God for not being able to control me, a miserable, lonely, wretched creature." When free choice is misused, that is, when the self chooses to be something other than itself, freedom becomes enslavement, as the self finds itself in bondage to itself and to its own misused freedom.

Finally, it is possible to think of Christ as our freedom, and yet to disregard free choice. Religious thinkers who quote the gospel saying "you shall know the truth and the truth shall make you free" may see themselves as advocates of Christ's freedom, but not freedom of choice. Charading as religious proponents of freedom, some people may say "in order to have God's freedom, you must be willing not to make any choices on your own." But this is essentially just one more way of escaping from freedom. It is no different than avoiding choice by submitting to a tyrannical leader, except that in lieu of a tyrant, one projects God as a master to whom one must submit one's will.

Kierkegaard's view of freedom does not ask one to abandon free choice to find freedom in submission. In 1834, when he was 21 years old and a decade before he wrote *The Concept of Anxiety*, Kierkegaard wrote in his journals "The concept 'predestination' must be regarded as a thoroughgoing abortion. Doubtlessly having originated in order to relate freedom and God's omnipotence, it solves the riddle by denying one of the concepts and consequently explains nothing" (*SKJP* 2, 1230). Religious thinkers who solve the problem of freedom by associating freedom with Christ and denying free choice do not solve the problem. Instead, Kierkegaard's solution to the relation between free choice and God's omnipotence preserves both elements by urging that a weak god could only create beings under the god's control, but an omnipotent God can make a free being, that is, a being that genuinely has free choice, for freedom is the greatest good, and only an omnipotent God could produce a being with this goodness (*SKJP* 2, 1251).[12] Human freedom, therefore, entails free choice.

4. *The Etymology of the Term Freedom.*

Further insight into the various aspects of freedom can be found in an examination of its etymology.[13] The Danish term "*friheden*" shares the same etymological root as the English term "freedom." The primary etymological sense of the term "free" is "dear, beloved." The roots of the English "free" and the Danish "*fri*" both come from the Old High German "*frī*," which stems from the Indo-European root "*prijos*" (dear, beloved) and is related to the Sanskrit "*priyás*" (dear) and "*priyā*" (wife, daughter). Likewise, there is a connection with the Old English "*frīgu*" (love) and "*frēon*" (friend). The German and Celtic meaning "not in bondage or subject to control from outside" comes from calling "dear" (*fri*) those members of a household connected by ties of kindred with the head. A free person is as a friend or beloved, one joined to another in mutual benevolence and intimacy.

The root is also related to the Old Norse goddess *Frigg*, the corollary to Venus in Norse Mythology. She is the wife of Odin. (In English, the sixth day of the week, Friday, is named after her.) Like Venus, she mythologically represents love and unconstrained devotion.

There is one other etymology that is worth noting, one that Kierkegaard mentions (*SKJP* 2, 1261). The Danish term "*frie*" means "to propose," that is, "to make an offer of marriage." This Danish phrase for betrothal captures both the sense of free choice and the sense of harmonious love.

So the root meaning of freedom includes the concept of love and devotion to a beloved. As a beloved, one chooses to be devoted and in the devotion one is free. The choice to be devoted to the beloved is made in freedom, that is, it is a free choice. The devotion to the beloved is itself freedom, that is, the freedom of right relation.

But as the word evolved, freedom came to be associated solely with choice. To the modern ear, "I am free" comes to mean simply "I choose" or "I can decide for myself." The Enlightenment promise of freedom continues to issue a soft sweet smell, for freedom still carries with it the hidden sense of loving devotion. The land of the free is originally thought to be simultaneous with the land flowing with milk and honey, a land where individuals live in right relation with themselves and with God. But the substance of freedom becomes lost with each bad choice, so that eventually freedom is disassociated from goodness and made synonymous with choice, any choice.

Hence the history of the word freedom reveals the key to the devaluation and revaluation of the concept of freedom. Freedom is rooted in loving devotion, in right relation. This care of the beloved entails a choice, and so freedom comes to mean the ability to choose. But as freedom is associated solely with choice, there develops a rejection of the content of choice. Eventually, one misuses freedom, one chooses not to choose, or chooses to be more or less than what one is. As the habit of misused freedom is compounded, freedom is celebrated, but merely as choice. Ultimately, as Kierkegaard writes, "emphasizing freedom of choice as such means the sure loss of freedom" (*SKJP* 2, 1261).

5. True Freedom

Given this analysis of anxiety and despair in Kierkegaard's writing, we can conclude that the fundamental meaning of freedom is the freedom of self-actualization. Freedom means, at its most basic level, to be oneself, that is, to live in right relation to oneself, to others and to God. It follows that an analysis of the meaning of freedom must begin with the psychological and metaphysical task of understanding what it means to be a self. Since we are selves, this task is not simply an abstract issue for erudite scholars, but is central to the existential and moral task facing each human being. And since we are sinful human beings, this task is clouded by sin and leads ultimately to a religious answer.

The analysis of the self offered by Kierkegaard results in this. To be a human being means to be a spirit, that is, a self. The self is a relation, a synthesis of body and soul, of the finite and the infinite, of the temporal and the eternal, of necessity and possibility. Yet the relation of the self is not an inert, stagnant relation, but a dynamic relation capable of self-awareness and choice. The self is capable of choosing to be itself or of choosing not to be itself. The self is a self among other selves, and a self in relation to God. When the self chooses to become itself, to live in right relation to itself, to others and to God, then the self is freedom. This actualization is the fundamental meaning of freedom.

This freedom of self-actualization entails freedom of choice. Since the self is a relation that relates itself to itself, it has the ability either to be itself or not to be itself. This freedom of choice is, when studied in isolation, neutral regarding the content of any particular choice. It does not itself provide a criterion for choice. Freedom of choice says "Any choice is possible, now choose." So freedom of choice, by itself, is not normative insofar as it does not provide any concrete criterion to determine if some choices are better than others. The criterion for choice is not found by focusing solely on free choice, but on the freedom of self-actualization. So the appropriate criterion for ethics is "Does this action put me in right relation with myself, with others and with God?" Hence, freedom of choice makes it possible for the self to lie, cheat, steal, murder, and exploit, while the freedom of self-actualization can be used as a criterion to determine that such actions are immoral.

Freedom of choice is a great good when used appropriately, for it puts the responsibility for one's relation to oneself, others and God within oneself. However, when freedom of choice is misused, it proves to be a great downfall, for it gives the self the ability to destroy itself spiritually.

If freedom of choice were the ultimate meaning of freedom, then MacIntyre's criticism would be accurate: Kierkegaard's ethics would be completely irrational and criterionless. An ethics of freedom whose only principle is free choice is nonsensical, for it cannot distinguish between good and evil. Murder, rape and the most immoral of acts can be justified, so long as they are chosen. Anything could be deemed moral, as long as one freely chooses it.

But for Kierkegaard, the fundamental meaning of freedom is the freedom of self-actualization. Free choice is entailed in this, but Kierkegaard's ethic of freedom says more than merely "do whatever you choose." Instead, his ethic of freedom says take responsibility for your choices, and choose the course of action that puts you in right relation with yourself, with others, and with God. Freedom of choice then, is a necessary but not a sufficient element in Kierkegaard's ethic of freedom.

Kierkegaard's notion of the freedom of self-actualization also results in several normative claims about the freedom from force's outside of one's control. For example, since freedom is ultimately to live in right relation to oneself, others and God, it follows that to constrain the actions of another unduly is to disorder one's relation to another, to treat oneself as something greater than what one is and to treat the other as something less. Likewise, one may be obliged to work to prevent unjust rulers from capriciously constraining the freedom of others. Therefore, Kierkegaard's criticism of the rights based approach of modern liberal democracies is not that there is no justifiable claim to freedom from undue constraints, but that there is a social tendency to overemphasize these freedoms so that the fundamental meaning of freedom is lost. The freedom of self-actualization does imply freedom from undue constraints by others. However, the freedom from undue constraints is entirely negative. Not only does it lack positive obligation, it provides no direction. Ultimately, if freedom comes to be associated solely with freedom from external constraint, the self is left either escaping its own freedom or defiantly misusing it. So the freedom from undue external constraints is a necessary but not a sufficient condition for true freedom.[14]

Finally, it might seem that the fundamental meaning of freedom for Kierkegaard is to be found in Christ. However, this is not quite accurate. It seems more accurate to say that self-actualization is freedom's fundamental meaning. However, because individuals have misused their freedom, that is, because of sin, Christ entered the world. As a man, Christ is freedom. He is a self, and hence He is a self in anxiety, a self with freedom. However, He is a self that never misused freedom, who always acted in right relation to himself, to others and to God. So in that sense, He is a model of freedom, as He is a model of a self-actualized human being. Additionally, Christ is redeemer. Through the forgiveness of sins, He offers individuals freedom from sin. Nonetheless, this is not a freedom from free choice. Redemption does not take away individual free choice, so even after one has been freed from sin through grace, an individual continues to have the possibility of misusing freedom. Christ's freedom is a redemption, an atonement, but it is not an escape from free choice. It is not as if in Christ we completely lose the possibility of misusing freedom. Even with Christ's redemption, the fundamental meaning of freedom continues to be the freedom of self-actualization. But in light of the Christian revelation, it becomes evident that after sin, self-actualization will only be possible with the divine aid of redemptive grace. This grace makes self-actualization possible, for it is Christ's atonement that puts one in right relation with oneself, with others and with God. It is not the abolition of selfhood, nor does it eliminate free choice.

True freedom entails free choice, but this does not mean that every free choice is a choice that frees. Because of misused freedom, to become ourselves in freedom we have need of redemptive freedom. This freedom frees us from our misused freedom, and leaves us again with the freedom to become free.

Notes

Notes to Chapter 1

1. Walter Lowrie, "Translator's Introduction," in *Fear and Trembling* and *The Sickness Unto Death*. (Princeton: Princeton University Press, 1941) 135. Also see Walter Lowrie, "Translator's Preface" in *The Concept of Dread*. (Princeton: Princeton University Press, 1944) vi.

2. See for example the new series of books under the general editorship of Mark Taylor on "Kierkegaard and Post-Modernism" that is being published by Florida State University Press.

3. There is a fairly detailed discussion of eternal and the spiritual in *The Concept of Anxiety*. See CA, 81-93. Also, in chapters 3 and 4 of *The Concept of Anxiety*, Vigilius describes the anxiety of individuals who are in sin. But individuals who are in sin are, as Kierkegaard writes, individuals "in whom spirit is no longer dreaming," that is, individuals who are not solely at the mental-physical level. Therefore, according to Kierkegaard, it is possible for individuals in whom there is a misrelation in the self which is not merely at the mental-physical level to be in anxiety. In other words, for Kierkegaard, it is possible for an individual to be both in anxiety and in despair at the same time. On Malantschuk's view, however, this would be impossible. Stephen Dunning has pointed out that Malantschuk's view on this point is incorrect. See *Kierkegaard's Dialectic of Inwardness*, (Princeton: Princeton University Press, 1985) 293.

4. See chapter three.

5. See chapter six, section two.

6. Also, see Elizabeth Morelli's treatment of anxiety in *The Affectivity of Moral Consciousness* (University Press of America, 1985), where she makes it clear that for Kierkegaard, anxiety is not itself an illness.

7. This is evidenced by the fact that Kierkegaard uses the term angest over twice as many times in *The Concept of Anxiety* as he does in all of his other works put together. The same is true of his use of *fortvivlelse* (despair) in *The Sickness Unto Death*.

Notes to Chapter 2

1. Kierkegaard used both of these spellings in his published writings, angest 317 times, angst 162 times. *Angest* is the spelling employed in *The Concept of Anxiety*, except in one instance. The difference seems to be purely lexical and not substantive. See Alastair McKinnon, *The Kierkegaard Indices*. (Leiden, Netherlands: E. J. Brill, 1973).

2. The term bekymring is used 12 times in *The Concept of Anxiety* to mean care or concern. There, it has no connotation of worry or anxiety.

3. The best solution is probably to translate *angest* as anxiety, *bekymring* as worry or concern, depending on the context, *plage* as torment, and *selvplagelsens* as self-torment. However, the context of the usage can vary the meaning of any of these terms.

4. As noted above, Kierkegaard used two spellings for this term: angest and angst. He used the two terms and their related grammatical forms (*angesten, angestens, angester, angesterne, angsten, angstens, angster*) a total of 723 times in his published works. Of those, 349, or almost half, are in *The Concept of Anxiety*. The work with the next highest number of uses is *Either/Or* with a total of 111 instances in both volumes together. The remaining works and the number of times that angest or one of the above mentioned variants is used are listed below in the order of most uses: 57 in *Edifying Discourses,* 43 in *Christian Discourses,* 27 in *Fear and Trembling,* 19 in *Sickness Unto Death,* 19 in *Stages on Life's Way,* 15 in *Works of Love,* 14 each in *Crisis in the Life of an Actress* and *Training in Christianity,* 11 each in the *Postscript* and *Judge For Yourselves,* 9 in *Repetition,* 5 in *Thoughts on Crucial Situations in Life,* 3 each in *The Concept of Irony* and *For Self Examination,* 2 each in *Prefaces, The Point of View for my Work as an Author, The Lilies of the Field and the Birds of the Air* and *Attack Upon Christendom,* and 1 each in the *Philosophical Fragments, The Present Age* and *The Moment.* See Alastair McKinnon, *The Kierkegaard Indices.* (Leiden, Netherlands: E.J. Brill, 1973).

5. For example, *The Concluding Unscientific Postscript* and *The Point of View for My Work as an Author.*

6. There is some disagreement over the translation of the term *opbyggelig*. The first English translations used "edifying," while

Hong has encouraged the use of "upbuilding." Hong's argument for "upbuilding" is that it is etymologically closer to the Danish term; his argument against "edifying" is that in English the term carries a pretentiousness that is not present in the Danish correlative. Etymologically, "edify" is related to edifice; it comes from the Old French meaning to build. Hence, the difference between edifying and upbuilding in contemporary English is primarily a difference in contemporary connotations. It may be that the term "edifying" has taken on pretentious connotations primarily through its association with somewhat pretentious devotional literature. Still, since Kierkegaard did not use the term *opbyggelig* with pretense, "upbuilding" is perhaps preferable.

7. Aristotle, *Nichomachean Ethics*, 1094b12 ff.

8. See chapter three, section one.

Notes to Chapter 3

1. For a discussion of Hegel's, Marheineke's, and Martenson's attempts to arrange all the academic disciplines, including psychology, dogmatics, and ethics, according to the dictates of an ontological logic, see Niels Thulstrup's *Kierkegaard's Relation to Hegel*, (Princeton: Princeton University Press, 1980) 351-55.

On the topic of the necessity of original sin, Hegel writes "In its instinctive and natural stage, spiritual life wears the garb of innocence and confiding simplicity: but the very essence of spirit implies the absorption of this immediate condition in something higher. The spiritual is distinguished from the natural, and more especially from the animal life, in the circumstance that it does not continue a mere stream of tendency, but sunders itself to self-realization. But this position of severed life has in its turn to be suppressed, and the spirit has by its own act to win its way to concord again. The final concord then is spiritual; that is, the principle of restoration is found in thought, and thought only. The hand that inflicts the wound is also the hand which heals it.

"We are told in our story that Adam and Eve, the first human beings, the types of humanity, were placed in a garden, where grew a tree of life and a tree of the knowledge of good and evil. God, it is said, had forbidden them to eat of the fruit of this latter tree: of the tree of life for the present nothing further is said. These words evidently assume that man is not intended to seek knowledge, and ought to remain in the state of innocence. . . The serpent was the tempter. But the truth is, that the step into opposition, the awakening of consciousness, follows from the very nature of man: and the same history repeats itself in every son of Adam. The serpent represents likeness to God as consisting in the knowledge of good and evil: and it is just this knowledge in which man participates when he breaks with the unity of his instinctive being and eats of the forbidden fruit. The first reflection of awakened consciousness in men told them that they were naked. This is a naive and profound trait. For the sense of shame bears evidence to the separation of man from his natural and sensuous life. . . The story does not close with the expulsion from Paradise. We are further told, God said, 'Behold, Adam is become as one of us, to know good and evil.' Knowledge is now spoken of as divine, and not, as before, as something wrong and forbidden. Such words contain a confutation of the idle talk that philosophy pertains only to the finitude of the mind. Philosophy is knowledge, and it is through knowledge that man first realizes his original vocation, to be the image of God. When the record adds that God drove men out of the Garden of Eden to prevent their eating of the tree of life, it only means that on his natural side certainly man is finite and mortal, but in knowledge infinite.

"We all know the theological dogma that man's nature is evil, tainted with what is called Original Sin. Now while we accept the dogma, we must give up the setting of incident which represents original sin as consequent upon an accidental act of the first man. For the very notion of spirit is enough to show that man is evil by nature, and it is an error to imagine that he could ever be otherwise. To such extent as man is and acts like a creature of nature, his whole behavior is what it ought not to be. For the spirit it is a duty to be free, and to realize itself by its own act. Nature is for man only the starting point which he has to transform. The theological doctrine of original sin is a profound truth; but modern enlightenment prefers to believe that man is naturally good, and that he acts right so long as he continues true to nature.

"The hour when man leaves the path of mere natural being marks the difference between him, a self-conscious agent, and the natural world. But this schism, though it forms a necessary element in the very notion of spirit, is not the final goal of man." (*The Logic of Hegel*, tr. William Wallace, Oxford, 1892, 54-56.)

2. He does not limit psychology to the study of human behavior, as do many 20th century psychologists.

3. See chapter two, section three.

4. See section seven of this chapter.

5. This point applies most clearly to the first chapter of *The Concept of Anxiety*, for in that chapter anxiety is studied as the condition for the possibility of sin. In chapters two through four, different types of anxiety are considered.

6. Hence, Vigilius is a libertarian in the freedom/determinism debate.

7. For a good overview of the material on this topic with which Kierkegaard was familiar see Niels Thulstrup's "Adam and Original Sin" in *Biblioteca Kierkegaardiana*, vol. 5. Niels Thulstrup, Ed. (Copenhagen: C.A. Reitzels Boghandel, 1980) 122-56. For a good summary of the different interpretations of the doctrine of original sin and sin as well as Kierkegaard's knowledge of these interpreta-

tions, see Lee Carlton Barrett, "Sin and Self Identity: Two Responses to Kant." Unpublished Dissertation, Yale University, 1984. (Ann Arbor: University Microfilms International, 1984), esp. 271 ff.

8. See note #1 from this chapter for an example of Hegel attempting to give a philosophical exposition of the dogmatic concept of original sin. This is not what Vigilius is doing in chapter one.

9. Ronald Green has recently done research on the influence of Kant on Kierkegaard on this point. Green argues persuasively that Kierkegaard was at least familiar with and had likely read Kant's *Religion Within the Limits of Reason Alone*. Some of Green's conclusions are presented in "The Limits of the Ethical in Kierkegaard's *The Concept of Anxiety* and Kant's *Religion Within the Limits of Reason Alone*" in *International Kierkegaard Commentary, The Concept of Anxiety*. Robert Perkins, Ed. (Macon: Mercer Press, 1986), as well as in "The Leap of Faith: Kierkegaard's Debt to Kant," *Philosophy & Theology* 3 (1989) 385-411. Green's argument is more fully laid out in *Kant and Kierkegaard: The Hidden Debt* (Ithaca, SUNY Press, 1992). For an interpretation that places Kierkegaard after Kant and Schleiermacher, see Philip Quinn, "Does Anxiety Explain Original Sin?" *Nous* 24:2 (April 1990), 227-44.

10. This problem is taken up again in chapter two of *The Concept of Anxiety*.

11. See note #1 for Hegel's account on this point.

12. See Kant's *Religion within the Limits of Reason Alone*, Tr. J.R. Silber, (NY: Harper, 1960), where on p. 36 Kant writes "In the search for the rational origin of evil actions, every such action must be regarded as though the individual had fallen into it directly from a state of innocence. For whatever his previous deportment may have been, whatever natural causes may have been influencing him, and whether these causes were to be found within him or outside him, his action is yet free and determined by none of these causes; hence it can and must always be judged as an original use of his will. He should have refrained from that action, whatever his temporal circumstances and entanglements; for through no cause in the world can he be said to be a freely acting being."

13. Freedom here means freedom of choice.

14. For example, Josiah Thompson refers to anxiety as a hypochondria. *The Lonely Labyrinth*. (Carbondale: SIU Press, 1967.) Olaf Hansen describes anxiety as "the homesickness of the human spirit" which

"reflects the alienated condition of the human spirit apart from its source of being." "The Problem of Alienation and Reconciliation: A Comparative Study of Marx and Kierkegaard in the Light of Hegel's Formulation of the Problem." Unpublished Dissertation, Princeton, 1956.

15. This is supported both by some Kierkegaard commentators who have a more accurate reading of Kierkegaard on this point and by some contemporary clinical psychologists. For an example of the former, see H. V. Martin, *Kierkegaard The Melancholy Dane.* (London: The Epworth Press, 1950), where he claims anxiety "precedes sin, but is not the cause of sin. [Anxiety] is not itself guilt, yet it is the psychological concomitant from which the leap is made from innocence to guilt" (83). For an example of the latter, see John G. Finch, "The Message of Anxiety," in *A Christian Existential Psychology.* Ed. H. Newton Maloney. (Washington, D. C.: University Press of America, 1980) 172. Finch argues from a clinical point of view that anxiety is not in any way a neurosis — though it may be managed neurotically.

16. Much of the material in this section can be found in my essay "Does Anxiety Explain Hereditary Sin?" *Faith and Philosophy* 11:1 (1994): 117-26.

17. Thompson puts forth this view. Also, Mark Taylor, in an unpublished paper presented at the Søren Kierkegaard Society Meeting in New York on Dec. 29, 1987, set forth the view that Kierkegaard's writings are to be interpreted in light of his relationship to his parents, in particular his mother.

18. This interpretation, that objective anxiety is social, was suggested to me by C. Stephen Evans in a personal conversation on Jan. 5, 1988.

19. Three types of objective anxiety constitute the subject matter of chapter three.

20. The fact that Eve sinned prior to Adam in the Genesis account is ignored by Vigilius.

21. Hence, while de facto sin may get worse and easier with each generation, this is not completely inevitable, since it is based on free choices.

22. In his book *Kierkegaard's Psychology*, Nordentoft incorrectly equates the anxiety of sin with sin. See Nordentoft 1972, xxi.

23. The self is a synthesis of the physical and the psychical. Since humans have a psychical aspect, we have the power of imagination.

24. See Thomte's note in his translation of *CA*, 247.

Notes to Chapter 4

1. Much of the material in this section can be found in my essay "Existential Despair in Kierkegaard," *Philosophy and Theology* 6:2 (Winter 1991): 167-174.

2. From the French: *De-* (without) *-espoir* (hope).

3. The Danish word for two is *to*. The Danish word for double is *dobbel.*

4. Kierkegaard used the term *fortvivlelse* 625 times in his published works. Of these, 351, well over half of all the occurrences, are in *The Sickness Unto Death*. The work with the next highest number of uses is *Either/Or* with a total of 88 instances in both volumes together. The remaining works and the number of times that *fortvivlelse* is used are listed below in the order of most number of uses: 39 in *Works of Love*, 38 in the *Concluding Unscientific Postscript*, 17 in the *Christian Discourses*, 16 in *Stages on Life's Way*, 13 in the *Edifying Discourses*, 11 in *Purity of Heart*, 7 in *Thoughts on Crucial Situations in Life*, 5 in *Fear and Trembling, Repetition, The Present Age*, and *Training in Christianity*, 4 in *The Concept of Anxiety* and *The Gospel of Suffering*, 3 in *The Concept of Irony, Two Discourses at the Communion on Fridays, Point of View* and *The Instant*, 2 in *Judge for Yourselves*, and 1 in *For Self-Examination*. See Alastair McKinnon, *The Kierkegaard Indices*. (Leid, Netherlands: E.J. Brill, 1973).

5. For example, see the fourth version of the story of Abraham in the beginning of *FT.*

6. See Hong's "Historical Introduction" in *SUD*, xiv ff. Hong gives a succinct yet thorough historical account of the writing and publishing of *The Sickness Unto Death*.

7. Specifically, *Concluding Unscientific Postscript*, (1846) *Philosophical Fragments* (1844), and *De Omnibus Dubitandum Est*, which Kierkegaard never published, but which has since been translated into English and published.

8. The lower pseudonyms include all the authors of pseudonymous works up to the *CUP.*

9. Besides Anti-Climacus, the higher pseudonyms include H.H., the pseudonymous author of *Two Minor Ethical-Religious Essays*. The works by Anti-Climacus are the only ones that Kierkegaard describes as awakening.

Notes to Chapter 5

1. John 11:14.
2. Much of the material in this section can be found in my essay "Kierkegaard on the Self and Despair," in *Proceedings of the American Catholic Philosophical Association* 62 (1988): 106-115.
3. Paul Dietrichson interprets the passage by relating parts of it to characters in *Either/Or* and *Stages*. However, he ends up overemphasizing the similitude between the Judge and Anti-Climacus. Dietrichson makes too little mention of the religious character of Antic-Climacus's concept of the self. See Paul Dietrichson, "Kierkegaard's Concept of the Self," *Inquiry*, 8 (Spring 1965):1-32. Both Mark Taylor and John Elrod have extended analyses of Kierkegaard's concept of the self using the opening passage of *The Sickness Unto Death*. However, both have deficiencies. Neither adequately shows the relationship between despair and the self in this passage. Also, the role of the three spheres of existence in the passage has been underplayed and hence the essentially religious character of the self is not sufficiently accented in their analyses. Finally, they tend to focus on the first several paragraphs in the passage. This is helpful insofar as the first several paragraphs are surely the most difficult. However, they discontinue their analysis of the passage before the discussion of despair. Hence, they do not show the relationship between the self and the sickness unto death (despair), and this is the goal of the passage. Nor do they make clear that the opening passage is a summary of the entire work. See Mark Taylor, *Kierkegaard's Pseudonymous Authorship* (Princeton: Princeton University Press, 1980) 86ff., and John Elrod, *Being and Existence in Kierkegaard's Pseudonymous Works* (Princeton: Princeton University Press, 1975) 29-71. Also see William H.K. Narum, "The Concept of the Self in Søren Kierkegaard," *Univ. College J.* 10 1-29. H.A. Nielsen, "The Anatomy of Self in Kierkegaard," *Proceedings of the American Catholic Philosophical Association*, 52 (1978): 197-203. Robert Perkins, "The Constitution of the Self in Hegel's *Phenomenology of Spirit* and in Kierkegaard's *Sickness Unto Death,*" in *Method and Speculation in Hegel's Phenomenology.* Ed. Merold Westphal. (New Jersey: Humanities Press, 1982) 95-107. Ingmar Pörn, "Kierkegaard and the Study of the Self," *Inquiry*, 27, (1984): 199-205. For another interpretation of this passage, see Patrick Goold, *Faith and Philosophy*, 4:3 (July 1987):

304-318. For an interpretation that draws out social aspects of the self, (though perhaps twists Kierkegaard's intended meaning) see Stephen Crites, "The Sickness Unto Death: A Social Interpretation," in *Foundations of Kierkegaard's Vision of Community: Religion, Ethics, and Politics in Kierkegaard.* Eds. George B. Connell and C. Stephen Evans. (New Jersey: Humanities Press, 1992).

4. Chapter four, section one.

5. This point is important for my thesis on the relationship between anxiety and despair as well as for the theological relationship between sin and original sin. If it is the case that children are born into despair as a structural misrelation of the self, then they are born into sin and thus do not bring about sin for themselves through any choices they make. Such a view undercuts the whole analysis of sin and anxiety in *The Concept of Anxiety.*

6. Cf. Kafka's "The Country Doctor," in *Selected Short Stories of Franz Kafka.* Tr. Willa and Edwin Muir. (New York: Modern Library, 1952).

7. This is because despair before God is sin. Since orthodox Christianity claims Christ is without sin, he would also have to be without despair in the technical sense employed by Anti-Climacus.

8. The possibility of despair is universal in the strict sense, though the actuality of despair is not.

9. See the sections titled "Infinitude's Despair is to Lack Finitude" and "Possibility's Despair is to Lack Necessity."

10. See especially the "Diapsalmata" and "The Unhappiest Man" in *E/O I.*

11. The young man in *SLW* represents the melancholy that comes from indecision regarding life's possibilities.

12. See the sections titled "Finitude's Despair is to Lack Infinitude" and "Necessity's Despair is to Lack Possibility."

13. The correlate in *The Concept of Anxiety* is spiritlessness.

14. See chapter three, section five.

15. Chapter three, section seven.

Notes to Chapter 6

1. This is explained below in section four.

2. This is explained below in section six.

3. The discussion of the relationship between despair and dizziness has misled several commentators, particularly Hong and Malantschuk, to think that despair is an intensification of anxiety. See chapter one, section two.

4. The relationship of anxiety and despair to spiritlessness will be examined below in section five.

5. This passage has been misunderstood by Malantschuk. He does not adequately account for the essential difference between the two. See my introduction, section two.

6. Chapter three, section two.

7. See chapter five, section five.

8. The Danish term for dizziness is *svimmelhed.* It can also mean faintness or giddiness.

9. This is the subtitle of *The Concept of Anxiety.* See chapter three, section one.

10. *Pap.* VIII 170:7. See *SUD*, 148.

11. Chapter three, section two.

12. Chapter five, section seven.

13. The psychologist Rollo May follows Kierkegaard on the relationship between anxiety and despair on this point and tries to locate when this occurs in human development. See Rollo May, *The Meaning of Anxiety.* (New York: W.W. Norton & Co., 1977) 39. He claims that based on his research, this usually occurs between the ages of one and three. Kierkegaard never takes up the same question. Further, Kierkegaard's method, at least as it is presented in *The Concept of Anxiety* and *The Sickness Unto Death* does not lend itself to answering this sort of a question. The method used by Kierkegaard is based on self-reflection. The method that must be used to answer May's question is based on the psychological observation of the behavior of others. As a point of speculation, Kierkegaard might agree with May's appraisal of when in human development people usually first wrongfully use their freedom. However, it should be made clear that Kierkegaard is suspicious of this kind of a question because it lends itself to the interpretation that this is simply a normal stage in human development. However, when the misuse of freedom is made into a stage in human

development, two things tend to occur at the theoretical level. First, the individual is no longer held responsible for the act, since it can be accounted for developmentally. Second, freedom is lost, since the individual's experience of anxiety and freedom is not adequately included in the psychologist's observation.

14. See chapter three, section five and chapter five, section six.

15. Kresten Nordentoft misses this point (Nordentoft 1972, xxi).

Notes to Chapter 7

1. The Danish term for free is *fri*; freedom is *frihed*. Kierkegaard used the term *frihed* (or closely related variants such as *friheds*, *friheden*, *frihhedens*, etc.) a total of 454 times in his published writings. Of those, 136 are in *The Concept of Anxiety*, while only five are in *The Sickness Unto Death*. The term *fri* (or *Fri*) is used 258 times in Kierkegaard's published writings, of which five are in *The Concept of Anxiety*. See Alastair McKinnon, *The Kierkegaard Indices*. (Leiden: E.J. Brill, 1971).

2. For other studies of the concept of freedom in Kierkegaard, see Jörg Disse, *Kierkegaards Phänomenologie der Freiheitsefahrung*. (Freiburg: Alber, 1991). Disse emphasizes the dialectic between autonomy and dependence. Louis Pojman's unpublished dissertation "The Dialectic of Freedom in the Thought of Søren Kierkegaard" (Unpublished dissertation, Graduate Theological Union, 1972) stresses two types of freedom in Kierkegaard: freedom of the will and freedom as redemption. (Pojman also wrote a separate dissertation on Kierkegaard at Oxford). Some of the idea's from Pojman's dissertation on freedom in Kierkegaard are presented in his essay "Kierkegaard on Freedom and the *Scala Paradisi*," *International Journal of Philosophy of Religion*, 18 (1985): 141-8. Also see Jean Wahl, "Freedom and Existence in Some Recent Philosophies," *Philosophy and Phenomenological Research*, 8 (1948): 538-56; Roy Amore and John Elrod, "From Ignorance to Knowledge: A Study in the Kierkegaardian and Theravāda Buddhist Notions of Freedom," *Union Seminary Quarterly Review*, 26:1 (1970): 59-79; Regin Prenter, "The Concept of Freedom in Sartre Against a Kierkegaardian Background," *Dialog* 7 (1968): 132-37, David Roberts, "Faith and Freedom in Existentialism: A Study of Kierkegaard and Sartre," *Theology Today* 8:4 (1952): 469-82; Masaru Otani, "Self Manifestation of Freedom in "Anxiety" by Kierkegaard," *Orbis Litterarum* 22 (1963): 393-98. For a study of Kierkegaard on choice, see Régis Jolivet, "Kierkegaard et la liberté de choix," *Orbis Litterarum* 10 (1955): 107-11.

3. For a discussion of the relationship between freedom from external constraint and political freedom, see Anthony Flew, "The Philosophy of Freedom," *Journal of Liberal Studies*, vol. 9, (1989): 69-80.

4. As I show below, "real" freedom refers to the freedom of self-actualization.

5. Bruce Kirmmse details how Kierkegaard's Denmark was an example of the move to modernity in microcosm. See Kirmmse's *Kierkegaard*

in Golden Age Denmark, (Bloomington: Indiana University Press, 1990), especially part one.

6. See Robert Bellah, et al., *Habits of the Heart,* (New York, Harper and Row, 1985). One of the main themes of Bellah's work is that an overemphasis on individual freedom results in moral breakdown.

7. See Bellah's interpretation of the biblical and republican traditions. In each, Bellah claims that freedom is fundamentally social cohesion, a community in right relation.

8. For studies on Kierkegaard's views on politics, see John Elrod's *Kierkegaard and Christendom* (Princeton: Princeton University Press, 1981), David Fletcher's *Social and Political Perspectives in the Thought of Søren Kierkegaard* (Washington: University Press of America, 1982), and Knud Rasmussen, "Søren Kierkegaard's Political Ideas" (Unpublished Dissertation, Rutgers, 1964). Also see Bruce Kirmmse, *Kierkegaard in Golden Age Denmark* (Bloomington: Indiana University Press, 1990).

9. *The Encyclopedia of Philosophy,* ed. Paul Edwards. (New York: Macmillan Publishing Co., 1967), volume four, 336ff.

10. See the last chapter, titled "A Corrective: The Solitary Self," in Mark Taylor, *Kierkegaard's Pseudonymous Authorship.* Taylor does a good job laying out this and related problems in Kierkegaard.

11. For a sample of Kierkegaard scholars trying to grapple with the place of ethics and politics in the individualism of Kierkegaard, see Foundations of Kierkegaard's *Vision of Community: Religion, Ethics, and Politics in Kierkegaard.* Ed. George B. Connell and C. Stephen Evans. (New Jersey: Humanities Press, 1992). In particular, I have found Merold Westphals's essay very insightful.

12. This is an excellent journal entry. It helps explain Kierkegaard's insistence on free choice without abandoning the idea of God's omnipotence.

13. Many of the ideas in this section can be found in my essay "Liberty is a Lady" in *First Things* 46 (October 1994) 18-22.

14. This is particularly so when applied to how one ought to treat others. It is not so clear that Kierkegaard would say that it is impossible to find true freedom under an unjust dictator. Insofar as one cannot control the actions of the dictator, one is responsible only for how one treats others, not how one is treated. So given this analysis of freedom, it is impossible to find true freedom as a tyrant, though it may not be impossible while under the rule of a tyrant. In a sinful world, each individual's task is to see that true freedom begins with oneself.

BIBLIOGRAPHY

Primary Sources

Kierkegaard, Søren. *The Concept of Anxiety.* Reidar Thomte and Albert B. Anderson, trans. Princeton: Princeton University Press, 1980.

_____. *The Sickness Unto Death.* Howard and Edna Hong, trans. Princeton: Princeton University Press, 1980.

* * *

_____. *Samlede Værker.* Ed. by A. B. Drachmann, J. L. Heiberg, and A. O. Lange. Supervised by Peter P. Rohde, 20 vols. Copenhagen: Gyldendal, 1962-64.

* * *

_____. *Attack Upon "Christendom."* Walter Lowrie, trans. Princeton: Princeton University Press, 1968.

_____. *Christian Discourses.* Walter Lowrie, trans. Princeton: Princeton University Press, 1968.

_____. *The Concept of Dread.* Walter Lowrie, trans. Princeton: Princeton University Press, 1946.

_____. *The Concept of Irony.* Lee M. Capel, trans. Bloomington: Indiana University Press, 1968.

_____. *Concluding Unscientific Postscript.* David F. Swenson and Walter Lowrie, trans. Princeton: Princeton University Press, 1941.

_____. *Concluding Unscientific Postscript.* Howard and Edna Hong, trans. Princeton: PrincetonUniversity Press, 1992.

_____. *Edifying Discourses,* 4 vols. David Swenson and Lillian Swenson, trans. Minneapolis: Augsburg Publishing House, 1943-1962.

_____. *Either/Or,* vol. I. David F. and Lillian Marvin Swenson, trans., vol. II, Walter Lowrie, trans. Princeton: Princeton University Press, 1971.

_____. *Either/Or,* 2 vols. Howard and Edna Hong, trans. Princeton: Princeton University Press, 1987.

_____. *Fear and Trembling.* Howard V. Hong and Edna H. Hong, trans. Princeton: Princeton University Press, 1983.

_____. *Fear and Trembling* and *The Sickness Unto Death.* Walter Lowrie, trans. Princeton: Princeton University Press, 1941.

_____. *The Gospel of Suffering.* David F. Swenson, et al., trans. Minneapolis: Augsburg Pub., 1947.

_____. *Johannes Climacus or, De Omnibus Dubitandum Est and A Sermon.* T.H. Croxall, trans. Stanford: Stanford University Press, 1967.

_____. *Journals and Papers.* Ed. and trans. by Howard and Edna Hong, Bloomington, Indiana: Indiana University Press, 1967.

_____. *Philosophical Fragments.* David F. Swenson, trans., rev. Howard V. Hong, Princeton: Princeton University Press, 1962.

_____. *The Point of View of My Work as an Author: A Report to History.* Walter Lowrie, trans. New York: Harper Torchbooks, 1962.

_____. *Prefaces: Light Reading for Certain Classes as the Occasion may Require.* William McDonald, trans. Tallahassee: Florida State University Press, 1988.

_____. *Purity of Heart is to Will One Thing.* Douglas V. Steere, trans. New York: Harper Torchbooks, 1948.

_____. *Repetition.* Walter Lowrie, trans. New York: Harper & Row, 1964.

_____. *The Sickness Unto Death.* Alastair Hannay, trans. New York: Viking Penguin, 1989.

_____. *Stages on Life's Way.* Walter Lowrie, trans. Princeton: Princeton University Press, 1957.

_____. *Training in Christianity.* Walter Lowrie, trans. Princeton: Princeton University Press, 1944.

_____. *Works of Love.* David F. Swenson, trans. Princeton: Princeton University Press, 1946.

Secondary Works

Accard Couchoud, Marie-Thérèse. *Kierkegaard Ou L'Instant Paradoxal.* Paris: Les Éditions du Cerf, 1981. Esp. chapters 1-5.

Adler, Mortimer. *The Idea of Freedom.* Garden City, NY: Doubleday, 1958.

Allen, E.L. *Existentialism from Within.* Westport, CN: Greenwood Press, 1974. Esp. chapter three, "Man and His Freedom."

Amore, Roy, and Elrod, John. "From Ignorance to Knowledge: A Study in the Kierkegaardian and Theravada Buddhist Notions of Freedom." *Union Seminary Quarterly Review* 26 (1970): 59-79.

Arbaugh, George B. and Arbaugh, George E. *Kierkegaard's Authorship.* London: George Allen & Unwin Ltd., 1968.

Aristotle, *Nichomachean Ethics.* Tr. Terence Irwin, Indianapolis: Hackett, 1985.

Augustine. *Confessions.* Tr. John K. Ryan, Garden City, NY: Doubleday, 1960.

Barrett, Lee. "Kierkegaard's Anxiety and the Augustinian Doctrine of Original Sin," *International Kierkegaard Commentary: The Concept of Anxiety,* ed. R. Perkins, Macon, Georgia: Mercer University Press, 1985, 35-62.

_____. Sin and Self Identity: Two Responses to Kant. Dissertation, Yale University, 1984.

Beabout, Gregory R. "Does Anxiety Explain Hereditary Sin?" *Faith and Philosophy* 11:1 (1994): 117-26.

_____, "Existential Despair in Kierkegaard." *Philosophy and Theology* 6 (1991): 167-74.

_____. "Kierkegaard on the Self and Despair: An Analysis of the Opening Passage of The Sickness Unto Death." *Proceedings of the American Catholic Philosophical Association.* 62 (1988): 106-15.

_____. "Liberty is a Lady" in *First Things* 46 (October 1994): 18-22.

Becker, Ernest. *The Denial of Death*. New York: MacMillan, 1973.

Bellah, Robert, et al. *Habits of the Heart*. New York, Harper and Row, 1985.

Berthold, Fred. "Review of The Concept of Anxiety", in *Religious Studies*. (1982): 406-08.

Bykhovski, Bernard. "A Philosophy of Despair," *Philosophy and Phenomenological Research* 34 (1973): 187-200.

Carr, Charles. "Kierkegaard on Guilt," *Journal of Psychology and Theology* 13 (1973): 15-21.

Clive, Geoffrey. "The Sickness Unto Death in the Underworld: A Study in Nihilism," *Harvard Theological Review* 51 (1958): 135-67.

Coe, David K. *Angst and the Abyss: the Hermeneutics of Nothingness*. Chico: Scholars Press, 1985.

Cole, J. Preston. Kierkegaard's Concept of Dread with Constant Reference to Sigmund Freud. Dissertation, Drew University, 1964.

_____. *The Problematic Self in Kierkegaard and Freud*. New Haven: Yale University Press, 1971.

Collins, James. *The Mind of Kierkegaard*. Princeton: Princeton University Press, 1983.

Connell, George B. and C. Stephen Evans, eds. *Foundations of Kierkegaard's Vision of Community: Religion, Ethics, and Politics in Kierkegaard*. New Jersey: Humanities Press, 1992.

Crites, Stephen. "The Sickness Unto Death: A Social Interpretation," in *Foundations of Kierkegaard's Vision of Community: Religion, Ethics, and Politics in Kierkegaard*. Ed. George B. Connell and C. Stephen Evans, New Jersey: Humanities Press, 1992.

Croxall, T. H. *Kierkegaard Commentary*. New York: Harper & Brothers, 1956.

_____. *Kierkegaard Studies*. London: Lutterworth Press, 1948.

_____. "Man's Inner Condition: A Study of Kierkegaard," *Philosophy, Journal of the Royal Institute of Philosophy* 22 (1947): 252-55.

Diem, Hermann. *Kierkegaard, An Introduction*. David Green, trans. Richmond: John Knox Press, 1966. Esp. pp. 51-60.

Dietrichson, Paul. "Kierkegaard's Concept of the Self," *Inquiry* 3 (1965).

Disse, Jörg. *Kierkegaards Phänomenologie der Freiheitserfahrung*. Freiburg: Alber, 1991.

Dunning, Stephen N. *Kierkegaard's Dialectic of Inwardness*. Princeton: Princeton University Press, 1985.

_____. "Kierkegaard's Systematic Analysis of Anxiety," in *International Kierkegaard Commentary: The Concept of Anxiety*. Ed. by R. Perkins, Macon, Georgia: Mercer University Press, 1985, 7-33.

Dupré, Louis K. *Kierkegaard as Theologian*. New York: Sheed & Ward, 1963.

_____. "The Constitution of the Self in Kierkegaard's Philosophy," *International Philosophical Quarterly* 3 (1963): 506-26.

_____. "Of Time and Eternity," in *International Kierkegaard Commentary: The Concept of Anxiety*. Ed. R. Perkins. Macon, Georgia: Mercer University Press, 1985, 111-32.

Edwards, Paul. *The Encyclopedia of Philosophy*. New York: MacMillan Publishing Co., 1967, esp. Alasdair MacIntyre's entry on Kierkegaard.

Ellul, Jacques. *The Ethics of Freedom*. Tr. Geoffrey W. Bromiley, Grand Rapids: Eerdmans, 1976.

Elrod, John. An Interpretation of Søren Kierkegaard's Concept of the Self in the Pseudonymous Corpus. Dissertation, Princeton, 1972.

_____. *Being and Existence in Kierkegaard's Pseudonymous Works*. Princeton University Press, 1975. Esp. part one.

_____. "Feurbach and Kierkegaard on the Self," *Journal of Religion* 56 (1976): 348-65.

_____. *Kierkegaard and Christendom.* Princeton: Princeton University Press, 1981.

_____. "The Self in Kierkegaard's Pseudonyms," *International Journal of Philosophy of Religion* 4 (1974): 218-40.

Evans, C. Stephen. *Søren Kierkegaard's Christian Psychology.* Grand Rapids, MI: Zondervan, 1990.

Finch, John G. "The Message of Anxiety," in *A Christian Existential Psychology.* Washington D.C.: University Press of America, 1980.

Fletcher, David. *Social and Political Perspepctives in the Thought of Søren Kierkegaard.* Washington: University Press of America, 1982.

Flew, Anthony. "The Philosophy of Freedom," *Journal of Liberal Studies* 9 (1989): 69-80.

Fromm, Erich. *Escape From Freedom.* New York: Avon, 1982.

Freud, Sigmund. *Civilization and Its Discontents.* Tr. James Strachey, New York: Norton, 1961.

Gardiner, Patrick. *Kierkegaard.* Oxford: Oxford University Press, 1988. Esp. chapter 6, "Freedom and the Self."

Gill, Jerry H., ed. *Essays on Kierkegaard.* Minneapolis: Burgess, 1969.

Gilmartin, Thomas. Soul Sickness: A Comparison of William James and Soren Kierkegaard. Dissertation, Graduate Theological Union, Berkeley, 1974.

Goold, Patrick. "Kierkegaard's Christian Imperative," *Faith and Philosophy* 4 (1987) 304-18.

Green, Ronald. *Kant and Kierkegaard: The Hidden Debt.* Ithaca: SUNY Press, 1992.

_____. "The Leap of Faith: Kierkegaard's Debt to Kant," *Philosophy & Theology* 3 (1989): 385-411.

_____. "The Limits of the Ethical in Kierkegaard's *The Concept of Anxiety* and Kant's *Religion Within the Limits of Reason Alone*," in *International Kierkegaard Commentary: The Con-*

cept of Anxiety. Ed. R. Perkins, Macon, Georgia: Mercer University Press, 1985, 63-88.

Grene, Marjorie. *Dreadful Freedom.* Later published as *Introduction to Existentialism.* Chicago, 1959.

Grimault, Magurite. *La Mélancolie de Kierkegaard.* Paris: Aubier-Montaigne, 1965.

Grimsley, Ronald. *Søren Kierkegaard.* London: Studio Vista, 1962.

Gwaltney, Marilyn E. The Concept of Alienation in Kierkegaard. Dissertation, SUNY Buffalo, 1976.

Hall, Ronald L. "Language and Freedom: Kierkegaard's Analysis of the Demonic in *The Concept of Anxiety,* in *International Kierkegaard Commentary: The Concept of Anxiety.* Ed. R. Perkins, Macon: Mercer University Press, 1985, 153-66.

Hamilton, Kenneth. "Kierkegaard on Sin," *Scottish Journal of Theology* 17 (1964): 289-302.

_____. "Life in the House that Angst Built," *Hibbert Journal* 57 (1958): 46-55.

_____. "Man: Anxious or Guilty? A Second Look at Kierkegaard's Concept of Dread," in *Essays on Kierkegaard.* Ed. Jerry H. Gill, Minneapolis: Burgess, 1969, 169-74.

Hannay, Alastair. "A Kind of Philosopher: Comments in Connection with Some Recent Books on Kierkegaard," *Inquiry* (1975): 354-365.

_____. "Hamlet Without the Prince of Denmark Revisited: Pörn on Kierkegaard and the Self," *Inquiry* 28 (1985): 261-71.

_____. *Kierkegaard.* London: Routledge & Kegan Paul, 1982.

_____. "Kierkegaard's Philosophy of Mind," in *Contemporary Philosophy,* Vol. 4, *Philosophy of Mind.* Ed. G. Floistad, The Hague, Martinus Nijhoff, 1983.

Hanson, Olaf. The Problem of Alienation and Reconciliation: A Comparative Study of Marx and Kierkegaard in the Light of Hegel's Formulation of the Problem. Dissertation, Princeton University, 1956.

Harris, Edward. *Man's Ontological Predicament.* Stockholm: Almqvist & Wiksell International, Uppsala, 1984.

Hartman, Robert S. "The Self in Kierkegaard," *J. Existent.* 2 (1962): 409-36.

Hegel, G.W.F. *The Logic of Hegel.* Tr. William Wallace, Oxford, 1892.

Heidegger, Martin. *Being and Time.* Tr. John Macquarrie and Edward Robinson, New York: Harper & Row, 1962.

Hoberman, John. "Kierkegaard on Vertigo," in *International Kierkegaard Commentary: The Sickness Unto Death.* Macon: Mercer University Press, 1987.

Hubbard, Benjamin J. and Starr, Bradley E. *Anxiety, Guilt and Freedom: Religious Studies Perspectives.* Lanham, Md: University Press of America, 1990.

Jaspers, Karl. *Karl Jaspers Basic Philosophical Writings.* Tr. Edith Ehrlich, Leonard H. Ehrlich and George B. Pepper. Athens, Ohio: Ohio University Press, 1986.

Jolivet, Régis. "Kierkegaard et la liberté de choix," *Orbis Litterarum* 10 (1955): 107-11.

Kafka, Franz. *Selected Short Stories of Franz Kafka.* Tr. Willa and Edwin Muir. New York: Modern Library, 1952.

Kainz, Howard P. "The Relationship of Dread to Spirit in Man and Woman According to Kierkegaard," *The Modern Schoolman.* 47 (1969): 1-13.

Kaltreider, Kurt. The Self, Existence and Despair in Kierkegaard: A Secular Interpretation. Dissertation. The University of Tennessee, Knoxville, 1977.

Kant, Immanuel. *Religion Within the Limits of Reason Alone.* Tr. J. R. Silber, New York: Harper, 1960.

Kirmmse, Bruce. *Kierkegaard in Golden Age Denmark.* Bloomington: Indiana University Press, 1990.

Künzli, Arnold. *Die Angst als Abendlandische Krankheit.* Zurich: Rascher Verlag, 1948.

Likins, Marjorie Harjes. The Concept of Selfhood in Freud and Kierkegaard. Dissertation, Columbia, 1963.

Locke, John. *Two Treatises of Government.* Cambridge, 1960.

MacIntyre, Alasdair. *After Virtue.* Second Ed. Notre Dame: University of Notre Dame Press, 1984.

Mackey, Louis. *Kierkegaard: A Kind of Poet.* Philadelphia: University of Pennsylvania Press, 1971.

Magurshak, Dan. "The Concept of Anxiety: The Keystone of the Kierkegaard-Heidegger Relationship," in *International Kierkegaard Commentary: The Concept of Anxiety.* Ed. Robert Perkins. Macon, GA: Mercer University Press, 1986, 167-95.

Malantschuk, Gregor. *Kierkegaard's Thought.* Ed. and tr. Howard V. Hong and Edna Hong. Princeton: Princeton University Press, 1971.

_____. *Kierkegaard's Way to the Truth.* Tr. Mary Michelsen. Minneapolis: Augsburg Publishing House, 1963. Esp. chapter 6, "The Dialectic of Freedom."

Martin, H. V. *Kierkegaard The Melancholy Dane.* London: The Epworth Press, 1950.

May, Rollo. *The Meaning of Anxiety.* New York: W. W. Norton & Co., 1977.

_____. *Freedom and Destiny.* New York: Norton, 1981.

McCarthy, Vincent A. *The Phenomenology of Moods in Kierkegaard.* The Hague: Martinus Nijhoff, 1978.

_____. "Psychological Fragments: Kierkegaard's Relgious Psychology," in *Kierkegaard's Truth: The Disclosure of the Self.* Ed. Joseph H. Smith. New Haven: Yale University Press, 1981.

_____. "Schelling and Kierkegaard on Freedom and Fall," in *International Kierkegaard Commentary: The Concept of Anxiety.* Ed. R. Perkins, Macon: Mercer University Press, 1985, 89-110.

McKinnon, Alastair. *The Kierkegaard Indices.* Leid, Netherlands: E.J. Brill, 1973.

Miller, Libuse Lukas. *In Search of the Self.* Philadelphia: Muhlenberg Press, 1962.

Morelli, Elizabeth A. *Anxiety: A Study of the Affectivity of Moral Consciousness.* New York: University Press of America, 1985.

Morris, T. "Kierkegaard on Despair and the Eternal," *Sophia* 28 (1989): 21-30.

Narum, William H.K. "The Concept of the Self in Søren Kierkegaard," *Univ. College J.* 10 1-29.

Niebuhr, Reinhold. *The Nature and Destiny of Man.* New York: Charles Scribner's Sons, 1945.

Nielsen, H.A. "The Anatomy of Self in Kierkegaard," *Proceedings of the American Catholic Philosophical Association.* 52 (1978): 197-203.

Nordentoft, Kresten. *Kierkegaard's Psychology.* Tr. Bruce H. Kirmmse. Pittsburgh: Duquesne University Press, 1972.

Ostenfeld, Ib. *Søren Kierkegaard's Psychology.* Tr. Alastair McKinnon, Waterloo, Ontario: Wilfred Laurier University Press, 1978.

Otani, Masaru. "Self-Manifestation of Freedom in 'Anxiety' by Kierkegaard," *Orbis Litterarum.* 22 (1963): 393-99.

Paci, Enzo. "Il Significato dell'introduzione Kierkegaardiana al Concetto dell'Angoscia," *Rivesta di Filosofia* (Bologna-Torino) (1954): 392-98.

_____. "Su due significati del concetto dell'angoscia in Kierkegaard," *Orbis Litterarum.* (1955): 196-207.

Percy, Walker. *Lost in the Cosmos: The Last Self Help Book.* New York: Washington Square Press, 1983.

Perkins, Robert L. "The Constitution of the Self in Hegel's *Phenomenology of Spirit* and Kierkegaard's *The Sickness Unto Death,* in *Method and Speculation in Hegel's Phenomenology.* Ed. Merold Westphal. New Jersey: Humanities Press, 1982.

_____. *Søren Kierkegaard.* London: Lutterworth Press, 1969.

_____, (ed.) *International Kierkegaard Commentary: The Concept of Anxiety.* Macon: Mercer University Press, 1985.

_____, (ed.) *International Kierkegaard Commentary: The Sickness Unto Death.* Macon: Mercer University Press, 1987.

Plato. *The Collected Dialogues of Plato.* Ed. Edith Hamilton and Huntington Cairns. Princeton: Princeton University Press, 1961.

Pojman, Louis. The Dialectic of Freedom in the Thought of Søren Kierkegaard. Dissertation. Union Theological Seminary, 1972.

_____. "Kierkegaard on Faith and Freedom," *International Journal of Philosophy of Religion* 27 (1990): 41-61.

_____. "Kierkegaard on Freedom and the *Scala Paradisi*," *International Journal of Philosophy of Religion* 18 (1985): 141-48.

Pörn, Ingmar. "Kierkegaard and the Study of the Self," *Inquiry* 27 (1984): 199-205.

_____. "On the Dialectic of the Soul: An Essay on Kierkegaard," *Acta Phil. Fennica* 32 (1981): 198-210.

Prenter, Regin. "The Concept of Freedom in Sartre Against a Kierkegaardian Background," *Dialog* 7 (1968): 132-7.

Quinn, Philip L. "Does Anxiety Explain Original Sin?" *Nous* 24 (1990): 227-44.

Rasmussen, Knud. Søren Kierkegaard's Political Ideas. Dissertation, Rutgers, 1964.

Ricoeur, Paul. "Two Encounters with Kierkegaard: Kierkegaard and Evil, Doing Philosophy after Kierkegaard," in *Kierkegaard's Truth: The Disclosure of the Self.* Ed. Joseph H. Smith, New Haven: Yale University Press, 1981. pp. 313-342.

Roberts, David Everett. "The Concept of Dread," *Review of Religion* 11 (1947): 272-84.

_____. "Faith and Freedom in Existentialism: A Study of Kierkegaard and Sartre," *Theology Today* 8 (1952): 469-82.

Rousseau, Jean Jacques. *The Social Contract.* New York: Hagner, 1947.

Sartre, Jean Paul. *Being and Nothingness.* Tr. Hazel E. Barnes, New York: Philosophical Library, 1956.

_____. *Existentialism.* Tr. Bernard Frechtman, New York: Philosophical Library, 1947.

_____. "Existentialism is a Humanism," in *Existentialism from Dostoevsky to Sartre.* New York: World Publishing, 1956.

Schalow, Frank. "Dread in a Post-Existentialist Era: Kierkegaard Re-Considered," *Heythrop Journal* 30 (1989): 160-7.

Schrag, Calvin O. *Existence and Freedom.* Evanston: Northwestern University Press, 1961.

Silver, Jeffrey Howard. Kierkegaard's Psychology of Health and Alienation. Dissertation, Graduate Theological Union, Berkeley, 1978.

Skinner, B.F. *Beyond Freedom and Dignity.* New York: Bantam, 1971.

Smith, Joseph H. (ed.) *Kierkegaard's Truth: The Disclosure of the Self.* New Haven: Yale University Press, 1981.

_____. The Dialectic of Selfhood in the Works of Søren Kierkegaard. Dissertation, Vanderbilt, 1977.

Sontag, Frederick. "Kierkegaard and the Search for a Self," *Journal of Existentialism* 7 (1966-7): 443-57.

Sugerman, S. "Sin and Madness; A Study of the Self in Søren Kierkegaard and Ronald Laing," *Drew Gateway* 41 (1970): 48-49.

Taylor, Mark. *Journey's to Selfhood: Hegel and Kierkegaard.* Berkeley: University of California Press, 1980.

_____. *Kierkegaard's Pseudonymous Authorship.* Princeton: Princeton University Press, 1975.

Thompson, Josiah. *Kierkegaard.* New York: Alfred A. Knopf, 1973.

_____. *The Lonely Labyrinth.* Carbondale: SIU Press, 1967.

Thomte, Reidar. *Kierkegaard's Philosophy of Religion.* New York: Greenwood Press, 1969.

Thulstrup, Niels. "Adam and Original Sin," in *Biblioteca Kierkegaardiana*, vol. 5. Ed. Niels Thulstrup. Copenhagen: C. A. Reitzels Boghandel, 1980.

_____, and Marie Mikulva Thulstrup. *Kierkegaard and Great Traditions*. Copenhagen: C. A. Reitzels Boghandel, 1981.

_____. *Kierkegaard's Relation to Hegel*. Princeton: Princeton University Press, 1980.

Tillich, Paul. *The Courage to Be*. New Haven: Yale University Press, 1962.

_____. *Perspectives on 19th and 20th Century Protestant Theology*. Ed. Carl E. Braaten. New York: Harper & Row, 1967.

_____. *Systematic Theology*. Chicago: University of Chicago Press, 1957.

Tweedie, Donald. The Concept of Dread in Kierkegaard and Heidegger. Dissertation, Boston University, 1957.

Unamuno, Miguel de. *The Tragic Sense of Life in Men and Nations*. Tr. Anthony Kerrigan, London: Routledge & Kegan Paul, 1972.

Wahl, Jean. *Etudes Kierkegaardiennes*. Paris: Vrin, 1949.

_____. "Freedom and Existence in Some Recent Philosophies," *Philosophy and Phenomenological Research* 8 (1948): 536-56.

Wyschogrod, M. *Kierkegaard and Heidegger*. London: Routledge & Kegan Paul, 1954.

INDEX

Adam, 39-43, 46-57, 59, 61, 127, 162-63, 165, 185

aesthete, 27, 73-74, 86, 88, 93, 103

aesthetic, 22-23, 26, 30-31, 78, 86, 93, 103, 147, 149

almindelighed, 99-100

alone, 50, 56, 137, 151
   before God, 148
   forgotten by God, 21
   In defiance of God, 111

Amore, Roy, 171, 175

angest, 15-19, 159-160, 181

angoisse, 16

Angst, 15, 17, 160, 176, 179, 181, 184, 186

annulled, 44

Anti-Climacus, 10, 27-28, 75, 77-107, 109-14, 116-121, 126, 128, 130-33, 141, 166-68

anxiety,
   about the good, 65
   and death, 20
   and despair, 4-8, 8-13, 115-34
   and inclosing reserve, 130-32
   and spiritlessness, 127-30
   and the absence of the consciousness of sin, 59-62

as a feeling, 47

as an ontological structure, 48

as explaining hereditary sin, 49-58

as saving through faith, 66-68

defined, 46

in works other than *CA*, 19-22

of sin, 62-66

role in overcoming despair, 132-34

translation of *angest*, 15-17

Arbaugh, George E. & George B., 12-13, 175

Aristotle, 26, 161, 175

atonement, 36, 68, 157-58

Augustine, 49, 90, 175

Augustinianism, 55, 57

Barrett, Lee, 164, 175

Becker, Ernest, 7, 176

Begrebet Angest, 16-17, 181

bekymring (worry), 16, 160

beloved, 19, 93, 98, 107, 109, 153-54

Bellah, Robert, 137, 172, 176

Carpocratianism, 67

DATE DUE

HIGHSMITH #45230

Printed
in USA